The
Snapshot
Photograph

George Eastman with a No 2 Kodak camera, 1890 —
a No 2 Kodak camera picture

The Snapshot Photograph

The rise of popular photography
1888-1939

Brian Coe and Paul Gates

Ash & Grant

Ash & Grant Ltd,
120B Pentonville Road,
London N1 9JB,
England.

First published 1977

The Snapshot Photograph text © Brian Coe and
Paul Gates 1977

Designed by Nicholas Maddren, Campion Design,
Baldock, Hertfordshire, England

Casebound ISBN 0 904069 13 3
Paperback ISBN 0 904069 14 1

Printed in Great Britain by
The Sackville Press Billericay Ltd,
Billericay, Essex, England.

Contents

Introduction

American locomotive, 1890

'SNAPSHOT n., shot taken with little or no delay in aiming; instantaneous photograph taken with a hand camera'. (Oxford English Dictionary)

Originally a shooting term, the 'snapshot' began to acquire a photographic meaning in the late 1850s, when the first instantaneous photographs were made. A writer in 1859 talked of 'snapping' the camera shutter at a subject, and in 1860 Sir John Herschel used the term 'snap shot' in discussing the possibility of a rapid sequence of instantaneous photographs for motion analysis. The phrase did not come into more general use until the 1880s, when instantaneous photography became more generally practical. Progressively the term came to be associated with photographs made with simple cameras by non-experts. In fact, for some it virtually became a term of abuse. Ask a professional or keen amateur photographer to show you his snapshots and observe his reaction!

In this book we shall not consider the advanced photography of the expert using complex and expensive apparatus, nor, for that matter, the deliberate use of simple cameras by sophisticated photographers in order to achieve a 'naive' effect. We are concerned only with the kind of photography within the scope of the humble box camera, or of the simple folding camera used by the amateur. Since such cameras were usually capable of making time exposures, our definition of the snapshot can be expanded to include such photographs. Indeed, it is not the length of the exposure but the intention behind the picture which distinguishes the snapshot: a photograph taken simply as a record of a person, a place or an event, one made with no artistic pretensions or commercial considerations. For the social historian such records have now become an invaluable source of information about the life and times of the ordinary person. Popular photography began in 1888 with the appearance of the first roll film box camera; this history traces the evolution of the snapshot camera and its photographs during its first fifty years.

Picture Credits

Miss Gail Freckleton, Eastman Kodak Company, 17 (above), 23 (below)

Mr Nick Graver, 12, 49 (top right), 116 (above)

International Museum of Photography at George Eastman House, 48 (far left, left)

Lt. Col. John Lawrence, 35, 129 (left)

The Marquis of Tavistock and the Trustees of the Bedford Estate, 11, 15 (right), 86 (right), 69 (far right), 86 (above)

Mr Frank B. Mehlenbacher, 23 (above)

The National Trust, 62 (above left), 73 (top right), 91 (above), 117 (top right)

Mr Donald C. Ryon, 6

The remainder of the illustrations are from the Kodak Museum collection. From the early 1890s until the Second World War, the advertising department of Kodak Ltd acquired many thousands of snapshot negatives from customers. Some were competition entries; others were sent in response to requests published in Kodak and other magazines. Many were sent unsolicited to the Company and some were taken by Kodak employees. Most are of a high technical quality, and they provide a unique and detailed record of ordinary people and their activities over half a century. This collection is now preserved in the Kodak Museum, Harrow, London.

1 The social background

Amid the clutter of small objects to be found filling cupboards and drawers in the average household, the ubiquitous snapshot must surely rank among the most commonplace. Snapshots are, after all, very much a part of most people's lives. They have been so for over three-quarters of a century. To say 'most people' means just that, for the taking and enjoyment of snapshots have been for this period of time the occasional activity of a wide spectrum of society. It would be difficult indeed to find any other pastime which has been embraced more democratically from its earliest days. Those days began in the nineteenth century when democracy, or at least the kind of material democracy we know today, was less of an accomplished fact. Yet despite social and economic inequality of a degree unimaginable today, the advent of the first really simple to use cameras and their associated processing services brought a new pastime into being. Photography became accessible to all and appealed equally to those in all walks of life.

To say that a new means of self expression had been placed suddenly into the hands of 'the people' would be to over-dramatize matters. After all, by the latter part of the nineteenth century, photography had become a well established craft, even though its potential as an artistic medium was only just beginning to be realized by a few. What the popularization of photography did achieve, however, was the opening of an area of creative activity previously closed to those without some talent for draughtsmanship. It did this by providing ordinary people, for the first time, with the means to make their own pictures, and it is what such ordinary people did with this new picture-making device that is displayed in this book.

But first, we must define our boundaries. We deal here with the period from 1888, when the first Kodak camera was placed on the market, to 1939, by which time most of the technological advances we enjoy in present-day snapshot photography had either been introduced or foreshadowed. Within this span of half a century many millions of photographs were made and by far the greatest proportion of these pictures were 'snapshots'. Something of the origin of this term has already been discussed; its scope is wider than might at first be thought, and it has been applied to several types of photography. Popularly, it is used to describe the kind of photograph made by people with no previous experience of, and no particular interest in, acquiring skilled photographic technique. Such people will normally use simple cameras with few adjustments, designed for just such an approach.

A typical cartoon poking fun at the snapshot photographer

A MAN AND HIS HOLIDAY SNAPS   By A. C. BARRETT
REPRODUCED BY COURTESY OF "THE PASSING SHOW."

The professional portrait photographer could seldom match the relaxed mood of the snapshot

Generally a snapshot implies a short, instantaneous exposure of 1/25th second or less, with the camera held in the hand. The word can also imply the spontaneity of a picture taken quickly and with a minimum of prearrangement. On the other hand, many pictures classed as snapshots show evidence of considerable preparation and arrangement of the subject, and some are made with longer time exposures, necessitating some firm support for the camera. Thus the word snapshot embraces 'time' as well as 'instantaneous' exposures, and a degree of spontaneity as well as some manipulation of the subject matter. Its essential characteristic is that it has been taken by the photographically untutored, motivated by the simple wish to record and perpetuate their life and times.

For many years this type of photography has been the butt of both professional and enthusiastic amateur photographers, many of whom regard the snapshot as beneath serious consideration. The subject has provided cartoonists and comedians with a continuing source of humorous material. These attitudes are no doubt based on the snapshooter's 'naive' approach to his subject and his lack of technical expertise, as well as the occasional ludicrous images which result. Superiority, scorn and humour notwithstanding, many millions of snapshots made with the simplest of cameras have brought pleasure and satisfaction to their creators. These pictures have been made without any pretensions to being other than plain and unaffected records of people, events and places. But despite their uncomplicated approach, many of these pictures also possess a visual and historical interest which has only recently begun to be appreciated by more than the few perceptive individuals who have always recognized their value.

The story of the rapid spread in popularity of snapshot photography between 1888 and 1939 is essentially one of the continual refining and

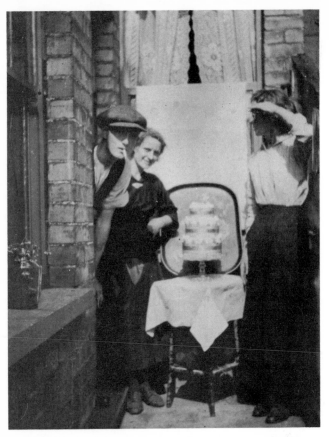

Two pictures taken in humble circumstances illustrate the snapshot's ability to record details of daily life seldom seen in more expert work

developing of one original notion. This idea was typical of the nineteenth-century pioneering industrialist's capacity for sensing the public's latent desire for certain goods or services and for supplying them at the right time. George Eastman recognized that there were countless thousands of people who would enjoy the opportunities of photography, but who were reluctant to involve themselves in the complex manipulations and chemical processes which the activity then demanded. By providing an internationally available processing service to develop and print the films exposed in simple, easy to use cameras, Eastman freed those who took the photographs from the need to learn the tedious techniques involved. From this time, snapshot photography grew apace, bringing about fundamental changes in attitudes to conventional photography. That these changes took place is incontrovertible; the merits of the pictures which helped to bring about the changes may be less obvious.

It has been said that our knowledge and understanding of people and events before 1839 would have been much greater had photography already existed. Few would contest this, but the statement might be better rephrased to specify *popular* photography rather than photography in general. It is through the snapshots made by generations of anonymous casual snapshooters, rather than from other sources of photographic illustration, that we enjoy in retrospect a view of the more informal aspects of the everyday life of the last ninety years. Just how much we owe to the snapshot and its unique view of the world of our forefathers is apparent if we compare it with other contemporary forms of the photograph.

Victorian photographs, apart from the snapshot, fall into two broad categories, amateur and professional. The work of the enthusiastic amateur photographer ought to provide a link between the snapshot and the professional photograph, but unfortunately it rarely does. With a few notable exceptions, the contributions from keen amateur photographers rarely included material of any real documentary significance. The early enthusiastic amateur was preoccupied, as many still are today, with the production of exhibition or 'salon' pictures. He aspired to create formalised 'camera studies', beautiful enough in their own way, but more concerned with evading contemporary reality than with portraying it. The exceptional few who chose to follow the path of realism have had their work well documented; the remainder have left little from the period between 1888 and 1939 which will merit serious consideration from the social historian. The 'creative' techniques by which compositions were 'elevated' — choice of lighting, angle and point of view, the manipulation of the camera and of the print in the darkroom — will frequently invalidate the picture as an historic record.

The snapshot, taken on impulse, perhaps almost at random, with no attempt to manipulate the subject or to wait for ideal conditions, may come closer to supplying the historian's needs. The talented amateur's failure in this respect is disappointing, since his freedom to photograph whatever he pleases with technical skill is his greatest asset. This freedom, fully exploited, could have left us a rich source of visual history; it has not, because most of these enthusiasts chose to apply their skills and equipment to the production of a seemingly endless series of 'picturesque' subjects inspired by contemporary academic painting.

The work of the professional photographer is diverse; the portrait photographer, by reason of sheer volume of output, deserves attention first. Professional portrait photographs tend to dominate any collection of nineteenth and early twentieth century photographs; they are usually the first to come to mind when the words 'Victorian photograph' are spoken. Assessed in terms of their documentary value, however, these portraits are necessarily limited in value. They have left us, it is true, with a precisely detailed record of the dress and fashions of their period. They also show us something of how their subjects looked when striving to impress with their wealth, their dignity or their beauty. How their subjects *looked*, mind you, rather than how they *were*. Of course there are exceptions, even among the most 'commercial' portraits of the time, and examples can be found where the photographer has penetrated the facade of genteel respectability to reveal something of the sitter's personality. Such pictures are, however, the exception, and most of the portraits preserve intact the 'Sunday best' image so dear to the middle and artisan classes who made up the majority of the sitters.

Snapshots too have always served as formal personal records, but for the modern historian they often provide a different kind of record and a different quality of information from the professional study. A brief glance through any snapshot album will reveal many pictures where painstak-

This snapshot of the Duke of Bedford and party in a light-hearted mood shows that not even the nobility were above face-pulling for the camera

ing efforts have obviously been made to set things up 'nicely', to make sure everyone concerned looked their best. The 'smile please' syndrome survives to this day. But the fact remains, that by reason of the circumstances of their taking, snapshots started out with a far better chance of truthfully depicting the character of their subject than the professional studio production could achieve. The casual circumstances of the snapshot, taken in familiar surroundings and in familiar company, could relax the subject and elicit a more natural pose and expression. Indeed, the snapshot made possible a new kind of informal portrait; freed from the constraint of the presence of the professional stranger, sitters could relax and adopt less inhibited poses. Moreover there was (and is) a strong tendency to 'clown' for the camera when it was in the hands of friends or relatives; mischievous attitudes and gestures became a temptation, as did the setting up of humorous set-pieces, often quite elaborate. Here was one facet of human personality, actually a remarkably common one, which had remained unrecorded until the snapshot camera simply and effectively provided the means.

The snapshot portrait also may gain an additional element of documentary value from the extraneous and 'irrelevant' detail which the professional photographer would have ruthlessly excluded from his portraits. Many snapshots which obviously started out as attempted portraits provide us with fascinating and evocative glimpses of the subject's environment: a corner of the backyard, a portion of ornate trellis imperfectly concealed behind the sheet erected as a makeshift background, a view through a partly open door

The ease with which snapshots could be taken encouraged the production of humorous tableaux

into a kitchen or drawing room. These details are often rendered more clearly than the principal subject, through deficiencies in technique! These 'faults', though unintentional, may nonetheless have historic value conferred on them by the passage of time.

The differences between the snapshot and the studio portrait also hold true for the snapshot and the professional news photograph. News photography became established at the end of the last century; much of the work of the new professional press photographer involved the recording of the great events of the time — wars, coronations, state funerals, jubilees, state visits and pageants. Whether of national or purely local importance, the resulting pictures bore the requisite air of formality and dignity, but few suggested any sign of personal involvement. A certain uniformity of approach is characteristic of the earlier news photographs. It was, after all, the event which mattered, and it had to be recorded as clearly as the circumstances and the lighting conditions

allowed. By definition, the commonplace and everyday event was not news, and therefore not recorded by the professional. Yet today such ordinary events have as much interest to us as the notable occasion, the importance of which has receded with the passage of time. The snapshot photographer could, and did, use his camera to record a new diversity of newsworthy events — to document a family wedding, to record a local pageant, to 'scoop' a dramatic scene happened on by chance or to photograph that great occasion over the shoulder of the professional man.

A slow and painstaking approach is evident in yet another area of the professional's activity — the production of 'local' views. These scenes, usually made for publication as picture postcards or as book illustrations, had their own special charm and appeal. Even allowing for the fact that they tended towards the more obviously picturesque aspects of the cities, towns and villages they portrayed, they were not without documentary value. But, as in contemporary portraits, it is the facade rather than the reality that we see. There is little insight into the kind of life being led by ordinary people in the places depicted. The snapshot's view of the urban scene can be quite different — back gardens, alleys and shopfronts are recorded for us along with main thoroughfares and civic monuments. Rather than including 'quaint' figures to suggest local colour, the snapshot shows people in their actual environment.

A certain reticence or impersonality in professional photography is hardly surprising. In the first place, these pictures were made for reasons entirely different from those of the snapshooter. The professional's task was, as it still largely is, to record for some commercial reason, to flatter, to sell. Secondly, the professional's background, training, and therefore his vision encouraged a traditional approach to the subjects he photographed. The cumbersome and heavy equipment at his disposal increased the need for formal ordering and arrangement, as did the limitations of the sensitive materials of the day. The combination of these factors imposed on the professional — or for that matter, on anyone attempting serious photography — a method of working which was both deliberate and slow, and which depended for its very success on a carefully controlled treatment of the subject.

The advent of the simple snapshot camera and its associated roll film, which offered the possibility of large numbers of pictures which could be made without reloading, brought about important changes in attitudes towards photography, and these changes came swiftly. It was almost as if the public had known all along the kind of photographs it wished for, but had never had the opportunity to make. The earliest surviving snapshots show evidence of a freer approach to photography which undoubtedly later influenced photography at large. The new camera encouraged people who had no previous experience to take up photography and to use it in new informal circumstances. The new photographers were free from the inhibiting constraints of the expert and they brought few preconceived ideas to their picture taking. Their choice of angle and viewpoint was free from the limitations imposed on the tripod mounted camera. Their very lack of expertise led them to tackle photography in circumstances and under conditions which the experts would have declared to be quite unsuitable, and yet they often succeeded in producing astonishingly effective results.

The snapshot provides, for the first time, a glimpse of how ordinary people of the late nineteenth century onwards lived, and records this with a factual accuracy and clarity which only photography can achieve. We see people at work and at play, on holiday or in the office; we see their houses, both inside and out. We can study the suburban garden and see the backyard as well as the front of the house. We can observe all those telling details which would not have been thought

From the beginning, snapshots show a fresh approach to photography

worthy of a picture in themselves, such as the kind of everyday domestic paraphernalia, now eagerly sought after by collectors, then in daily use and shown in context. Such subjects were inconceivable in the photography of an earlier era and it is in their recording that the documentary value of the casual snapshot can so often outlast that of contemporary photographs from other sources.

The importance of the snapshot as historical evidence is particularly crucial before the advent of professional photojournalism. Photojournalism began in the nineteenth century using bulky cameras and slow speed materials, but it only began to boom in the 1920s with the introduction of smaller and less obtrusive cameras with high speed lenses and using faster film. Even then its impact was limited. It was not until the coming of the popular illustrated weeklies such as *Life, Look, Picture Post* and *Illustrated* that photojournalism became the highly developed visual report and commentary on contemporary affairs that we are familiar with today. The photojournalist, unlike his precursor, the press photographer, turned his camera as much upon the ordinary and mundane as upon the great event or mighty person. By the end of the 1930s, photojournalism was recording professionally what, less than ten years earlier, had been almost the sole province of the amateur snapshooter. But the snapshot remains our prime source of visual information throughout the half century before the Second World War. Despite the explosion of visual media which has taken place in recent years, the documentary function of the snapshot continues to the present day.

Occasionally, snapshots produced images of remarkable beauty, perhaps by accident rather than design

If popular photography opened up a new area of cultural expression to the ordinary man and woman, to what extent can it be thought of as a form of modern folk art? Any examination of a large sampling of snapshots will reveal a surprising number of pictures which transcend the straightforward and mundane purpose for which they were taken. It is difficult to define the degree to which these pictures, their production motivated by the usual reasons of sentiment, record or souvenir, attain to something more. Folk art? If by that we mean an enduring value unselfconsciously achieved, then perhaps some snapshots may fall into this category. It is difficult to exclude the factor of nostalgia in any assessment of this sort, difficult because it forms a very large part of the appeal of the snapshot, but without doubt the practice of snapshot photography over the years has brought into being a large number of images which are attractive, even beautiful in their own right, regardless of the period or place of their creation.

This aesthetic quality of the snapshot has received less attention than it deserves, although this quality is no less interesting than its documentary value. The reasons for this neglect are neither hard to find nor surprising. Hugo van Wadenoyen, in his book *Wayside Snapshots* (1947), reveals a common attitude to pictures made with the simple camera:

'There are in this country alone some millions of snapshooters, but the vast majority of these have very simple cameras, which come into use only once or twice a year on special occasions such as holidays, weddings or family reunions. The snaps made in this way are nearly always dull and lifeless things. They are feeble ghosts of the occasions that have brought them forth, mildly evocative possibly to the imaginations of those immediately concerned in the events recorded but merely fatuous and boring to the outsider'.

Although an eminent professional photographer whose writing was distinguished by its intellectual flexibility, van Wadenoyen expressed an attitude towards snapshot photography which was typical of its day. It is an attitude which has by no means vanished. Lucia Moholy was a little kinder in *A Hundred Years of Photography* (1939): 'Though far from being really natural, these early amateur photographs had at least the advantage of being taken in natural surroundings, while studio portraits were being done without any or very little consideration for invidual attitude'. Kinder, perhaps, but the condescesion is still there. Is such an attitude justified? While we do not wish to attribute to snapshots qualities they do not, and possibly could never possess, the fact remains that many of them, nostalgic appeal apart, reveal a powerful quality of image, all the more remarkable since it is almost certainly accidental.

Some photographic historians have suggested that the snapshot has had a major aesthetic influence on workers in other graphic media. Although photography in general unquestionably did have a great effect upon painters in the nineteenth and early twentieth centuries, the kind of snapshot we are considering had little such impact during the period under discussion. Many artists have experimented with photography as a new medium; others have used it as an aid in their own work, but their approach to it has been that of the craftsman or experimenter. There is little evidence to indicate that the kind of snapshot imagery created by the public at large had any effect on them. Only in recent years has the visual language of the snapshot become a commonplace in the serious art world.

This language has remained surprisingly consistent over the years. The range of subjects covered by the snapshot has not varied greatly with time. Despite the technical advances which had been made in apparatus and materials, snapshooters at the beginning of the Second World War were covering much the same subjects as their predecessors at the end of the last century and, indeed, their successors today. Snapshot photography was primarily a leisure activity and basic patterns of human activity do not change as much as one would expect from the great material changes which have occurred. Thus the snapshot shows a continuing repetition of a few perennial themes, within which there can still be a considerable variety. Most snapshots fall into one of a few obvious categories. These may be broadly classified as people, leisure activities, seaside and holidays, the urban scene, transport, people at work, interiors and events. Representative samples of these subjects appear in the album section of this book, conveying the essence of the era in which they were made.

Not only do these pictures reflect changes in the popular approach to photography since 1888, but they also reveal a society undergoing more rapid and fundamental change than in any previous

fifty-year span. They show society's lighter moments, its 'off-duty' face, revealing so much more than its official one. The 'look' of any decade is well captured and preserved in the snapshots made in its time. Take, for example, the kind of image conjured up by the words 'The Twenties'. It is, probably, a composite, made up from half-remembered silent films, magazine illustrations or newspaper photographs, fashion plates from the period, or more recently, recreations for cinema, television or for advertisements. Compare this impression with snapshots of the period — perhaps some of those in this book. There will be a difference, because the snapshot shows us the world of the people and not that of the film-star, socialite or fashion model, and it is a difference for which the social historian must ever be grateful. To him the value of the snapshot will increase with the passage of time. Possibly at least twenty years must elapse from the time the snapshot is taken for it to begin to acquire historical interest. Ironically, this often coincides with the point at which its original personal values begin to decline. Few families today place any strong sentimental value upon snapshots after the passage of a generation. Perhaps an increased awareness of their potential usefulness may encourage those who have collections of such pictures to resist the temptation to discard them, in the interests of future generations of historians.

Two pages from photograph albums: right *of the Duchess of Bedford;* left *of a middle-class family*

2 'You press the button, we do the rest'

After the introduction of photography in 1839, its use was restricted at first to the professional, or to the amateur who was prepared to devote space and resources to the provision of a darkroom, and to acquire the necessary knowledge and skills to prepare, develop and print his negatives. The stand camera in general use was relatively bulky and heavy and a cart-load of equipment was necessary if working away from home. It was not until after 1871, when the gelatin dry plate was first proposed by a London doctor, Richard Leach Maddox, that commercial manufacture of photographic plates was effectively possible and by 1878 it was no longer necessary for the photographer to make his own materials. Gelatin dry plates were much more sensitive to light than those made by the earlier processes, which had required exposures of many seconds, or even minutes. In a good

The first Kodak camera, 1888

light, the new plates could be exposed in a fraction of a second, a time brief enough to permit the camera to be held in the hand and to allow the photography of moving objects. New camera designs appeared, capable of being used unobtrusively, and the term 'detective camera', coined by Thomas Bolas in 1881, was used to describe them. Some were disguised as parcels, hats, opera glasses or books; others were worn concealed under waistcoats or cravats. Some were of plain box form, undisguised but easy to carry. Although some were little better than toys, many were capable of good work. However, they all required that the photographer had access to a darkroom for loading and unloading the sensitive plates and for the subsequent developing and printing operations. Thus, while in the mid-1880s the snapshot was a technical possibility, it still required all the resources and skills of the enthusiastic amateur.

To simplify the process and thus bring it within the range of everyone, became the aim of George Eastman. Eastman, a bank clerk turned photographic manufacturer, had become one of the first makers of the new dry plates in America. His first step was to design, in collaboration with William Walker, a camera manufacturer, a roll holder by which a plate camera could be adapted to take pictures on long rolls of sensitized paper. The Eastman-Walker roll holder, introduced in 1885, was a great help to the enthusiast, but it did nothing to simplify the real problems which were inhibiting the more general use of photography. Eastman produced a 'detective' camera with an integral roll holder in 1886, but only made fifty of them, as they proved too expensive to produce. A second design proved much more successful. In 1888 he patented and introduced the Kodak camera, a small box form camera with an integral roll holder. It was sold ready-loaded with a roll of negative stripping paper film sufficient for one hundred circular pictures 2½ inches in diameter. A short focal length lens, of fixed aperture, meant that no focusing control was necessary and objects from a few feet onwards were sharply rendered. No viewfinder was provided, the camera simply being pointed at the subject and the 60° field of view of the lens allowed a considerable leeway. Later models of the camera were marked with V sighting lines along the top. Operation was simplicity itself. The shutter, of ingenious cylindrical form, was set by pulling a string, and released when ready by pushing a button. All that remained was to wind on the film, by turning a key, a revolving indicator measuring the required amount. A memorandum book was provided to record the details of the hundred exposures, to remind the user when the end of the roll was near. When the last exposure had been made, the camera was packed up and shipped to Eastman's factory, where it was unloaded, charged with a fresh film and returned. The exposed film was developed and printed and returned to the customer in about ten days. The most revolutionary part of Eastman's system was not the camera, but the concept of separating the operation of taking the pictures from that of developing and printing. The former could be done, as Eastman said, by 'anybody, man, woman or child, who has sufficient intelligence to point a box straight and press a button'. The processing could be done by specialists. Eastman devised the slogan 'You press the button, we do the rest' to sum up his system.

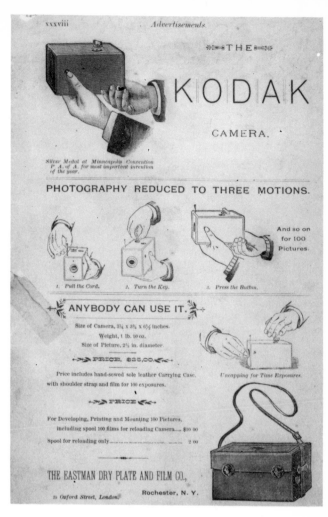

Above *An 1889 advertisement for the Kodak camera*

Below left *The Kodak camera took circular pictures 2½ inches in diameter*

Below *An excellent No 2 Kodak camera picture, taken in Rochester, New York, the town of its manufacture, in 1892*

A snap shot at Santa Claus.
Tommy tries an experiment with his father's Kodak camera.

Early Eastman pictorial advertisements; the bottom picture was captioned:
'Jack: *Do you think baby will be quiet long enough to take her picture, Mama?*
Mama: *The Kodak camera will catch her whether she moves or not; it is as "quick as a wink"* '.

In 1889 Eastman introduced the first commercial transparent celluloid roll film to replace the less satisfactory paper roll, and a larger No 2 Kodak camera, taking a 3½ inch circular picture. A new model of the original camera, with a new shutter design, was also introduced and designated as the No 1 Kodak camera. The following year Nos 3, 4 and 5 Kodak cameras were placed on the market, taking even larger pictures, up to four by five inches. To promote the new cameras Eastman advertised widely, not only in the photographic press in America and Europe, but also in leading magazines, such as *Harper's, Life, Time* and so on. Many of the advertisements featured young women with the camera, setting a pattern which was to become an integral feature of his company's advertising. In a promotional booklet, *The Kodak Camera*, Eastman outlined some of its possible uses:

'*Travellers and Tourists* Use it to obtain a picturesque diary of their travels.
Bicyclists and Boating Men Can carry it where a larger camera would be too burdensome.
Engineers and Architects Use it to record the progress of work in hand, and to note details of construction as they pass by.
Artists Use it to save time in sketching.
Parents Use it to photograph their children as they see them at play, not in the stiff attitudes of the conventional photograph.
Surgeons Use it to obtain a record of their 'cases', obtainable in no other way except at heavy cost.
Sportsmen and Camping Parties Use it to recall pleasant times spent in camp and wilderness.
Ocean Travellers Use it to photograph their fellow-travellers on the steamship deck.
Lovers of Fine Animals Use it to photograph their pets.
Anybody can use it. Everybody will use it.'

Eastman's optimism was justified, judging by the testimonials he received. 'Many single views and likenesses are worth to me far more than the cost of the outfit'. 'My first hundred pictures are highly satisfactory. Their excellence and beauty surpass my hopes even'. 'For a surgeon's use in keeping a record of cases ... it is invaluable'. Travellers and explorers were quick to see the possibilities of the new photography. The Arctic expeditions of Dr Nansen and Lieutenant Peary were equipped with Kodak cameras and rollable film, Peary bringing back with him more than two thousand exposures taken in Greenland.

However, others saw the snapshot camera as a mixed blessing. The musical comedian Corney Grain satirised the Kodak camera as 'an instrument of torture found in every country house. When you least expect it, you hear the dreadful click which is driving the world mad . . . Wherever you be — on land or sea, you hear that awful click of the amateur photographer, Click! Click! Click!' With the new camera came a new menace, reported in the *Weekly Times and Echo* in 1893: 'Several decent young men, I hear, are forming a Vigilance Association for the purpose of thrashing the cads with cameras who go about at seaside places taking snapshots at ladies emerging from the deep in the mournful garments peculiar to the British female bather. I wish the new society stout cudgels and much success, and wonder how long it will be before seaside authorities generally take steps to render bathing for both sexes decent, safe, and pleasant as it is on the Continent'.

Other manufacturers soon produced roll film cameras. In England Redding's Luzo camera, patented in 1888, took the Eastman roll films and enjoyed some success into the late 1890s. On the continent, the Prisma box roll film camera and the Cristallos folding camera were introduced around 1890. In America, the Blair Camera Company of Boston acquired the rights to the Englishman H. B. Good's patent of 1889, in which he described a roll film camera in which the film spools were placed just behind the front of the camera, the film being passed back through the focal plane and forward again. Blair's Kamaret camera, marketed in 1892, embodied this principle, making it a more compact form than that of Eastman's cameras in which the film rolls were behind the focal plane. Like Eastman, Blair offered a developing and printing service for users of his camera; soon, other concerns offered photofinishing facilities. One such firm in England was Thomas Illingworth (later to become a major manufacturer of photographic goods) who offered to 'Develop and finish Kodak and other film exposures quickly'.

All these early cameras had to be loaded in a darkroom, either by the supplier or the customer. To overcome this inconvenience, in 1891 Eastman introduced a new range of cameras, the A, B and C Daylight Kodak cameras. Superficially similar to those of the first generation, these new Kodak cameras differed in that the roll film was carried in light-tight cardboard containers. The film was wound through velvet-lined openings from one container to another, a length of black paper or cloth at each end protecting the film when loading or unloading. Although this new method did away with the need for a darkroom, it did not make as great an impression on the public as might have been expected. A neater solution to the problem was found by S. N. Turner of the Boston Camera Manufacturing Company. He proposed that the film should be attached to a longer length of black paper, wound on a spool with flanged ends, being thus completely protected from light when it was rolled up. Numbers printed in white ink on the backing paper could be read through a red window in the camera back, to locate each section of the film accurately, without the need for more complicated indicator mechanisms or exposure counters previously required. Turner's invention was embodied in the Bull's-Eye camera, first sold in 1892. Selling in several versions for around seven dollars, it was not an immediate success.

Eastman recognized in this new method the answer to his problem and in late 1894 began

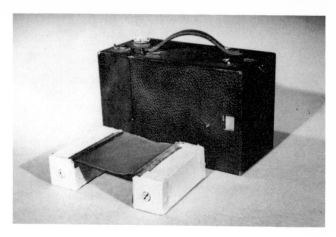

Top *The Daylight Kodak camera of 1891, with the film cartons which could be loaded into the camera in subdued light*

Above *The No 2 Bullet camera and the Pocket Kodak camera of 1895. These were Eastman's first daylight loading cartridge cameras, based on Turner's patent*

manufacture of the Bullet camera. When Turner received a patent for his invention in 1895, Eastman obtained a licence from him to continue manufacture; the new 'cartridge' roll film was so successful that in August 1895 Eastman purchased the Boston Camera Manufacturing Company and the patent outright. Although the Bullet camera, taking pictures 3½ by 3½ inches, was the first to be made by Eastman, the most successful by far was the tiny Pocket Kodak camera, launched in May 1895. The first to be produced by mass production techniques, the Pocket Kodak camera was a small box measuring 2¼ by 2⅞ by 3⅞ inches, taking a twelve-exposure roll film for pictures 1½ by 2 inches in size. It was a runaway success, demand outstripping supply from the very beginning. The output of three hundred cameras a day from Eastman's Rochester factory had soon to be stepped up to six hundred a day.

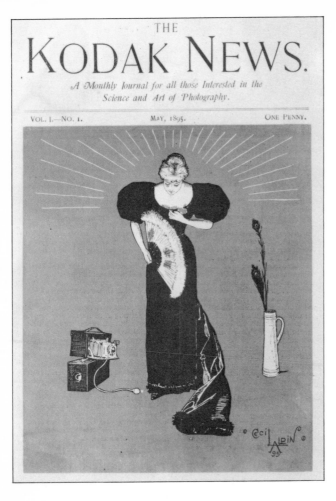

Top *The cover of the first issue of* Kodak News, *which appeared in May 1895, featured a highly stylized design by Cecil Aldin which reveals strong Crane and Beardsley influences*

Above *The Folding Pocket Kodak camera, 1897*

The first batch of three thousand Pocket Kodak cameras received in England were sold in a few days. The camera sold for one guinea, and a twelve-exposure roll film cost about two shillings to develop and print. In England the new cameras were publicised in a magazine *Kodak News*, the first of several publications intended to help the snapshooter to get the most from his camera. *Kodak News* was introduced in May 1895 and ran until August 1897.

The great success of the Pocket Kodak camera had shown that the public liked small cameras, but the pictures that it took, although of good quality, were small. In 1897 Frank Brownell, Eastman's camera designer and manufacturer, devised a camera which was, when closed, almost as small as the Pocket Kodak camera, but which opened up on spring loaded struts for use. Extremely compact when closed, the Folding Pocket Kodak camera took a picture 2¼ by 3¼ inches in size, introducing the format which was to remain the most popular snapshot size until the 1950s. It was the first of a range of folding cameras which was to prove enormously successful. The Folding Pocket Kodak camera was launched at a major exhibition held in London in November 1897. In April of that year the Eastman Photographic Materials Company Limited, of London, announced an international amateur photographic competition, with one hundred and thirty prizes amounting to almost £600. Entries could be sent to any of the major Kodak houses in England, France, Germany or America; they were restricted to photographs taken with the Kodak cameras and films. The response was tremendous; over 25,000 entries were received by the closing date, October 1. The competition was judged by Henry Peach Robinson, a leading pictorial and professional photographer, Andrew Pringle, a noted amateur photographer and a director of the Company and G. A. Storey, A.R.A. (substituting at the last moment for the President of the Paris Photographic Club, M. Maurice Bucquet). The organisation of the exhibition was in the hands of George Davison, a well-known pictorial photographer who had joined the Company as assistant manager in June 1897. He commissioned the designer and architect George Walton to create a striking decor for the exhibition, which was held at the New Gallery in Regent Street. As well as a display of many thousands of the competition entries, the exhibition included an invitation section, with work from leading pictorial photographers, a section of work by Royal photo-

Part of the great Eastman Exhibition, 1897. The first public exhibition of snapshot photography, with a decor designed by George Walton

graphers, notably Princess Alexandra, and a trade show of photographic apparatus. The exhibition was extremely successful; during its three week run it was visited by more than 25,000 people. The *Daily Telegraph* said 'Some of the competing pictures are gems . . . but the striking thing is the high average of merit, which means that hand-camera photography is far removed from toy-work, and that its influence in training the eye to appreciate points of beauty is greater than those who have never followed it would really appreciate'. The *British Journal of Photography* wrote 'One of the most remarkable photographic exhibitions yet held'. The *Manchester Courier* described the display as 'perhaps the finest that has hitherto been on view'. After its close in London, the exhibition moved to the National Academy of Design in New York, where its success was repeated, being seen by almost 26,000 people. The success of the exhibition was a measure of the extent to which snapshot photography had caught the interest of the public. Towards the end of 1898 the *British Journal of Photography* estimated that there were over 1,500,000 roll film cameras in use throughout the world. Although this is likely to have been a considerable over-estimate, it does indicate that the roll film camera had had extraordinary success in only a few years.

However, snapshot photography was still an expensive pastime. The first Kodak camera, ready loaded with film, cost five guineas in 1888, with a further two-guinea charge for developing and printing the hundred exposures. This would represent a month or two's wages for many people. Mass production had brought the cost of the Pocket Kodak camera down to a guinea in 1895, but even this was beyond the reach of many who might otherwise aspire to owning a camera.

3 The birth of the Brownie camera

Frank Brownell, Eastman's camera maker, had begun his career as a cabinet maker, turning to camera production in the early 1880s. His early productions were folding plate cameras of sound design and construction; because of the quality of his work he was retained by Eastman to manufacture the wooden parts of the Eastman-Walker rollholder in 1885. From this time until 1902 he was responsible for the manufacture of all of Eastman's cameras. He also designed and patented a number of the early Kodak cameras, notably the Folding Pocket Kodak camera of 1897. Eastman had the highest opinion of Brownell's abilities; in 1915 he said of him: 'He is the greatest camera designer that ever lived. Practically all the hand cameras are made after his designs today, throughout the world'.

Aiming to bring the snapshot camera within the reach of everyone, especially children, Eastman asked Brownell to design a very simple camera which could be mass produced for very low cost. The result was the Brownie camera, introduced in February 1900. Since the camera was especially suitable for children, Eastman had chosen a name which was a household word in America. The Canadian writer and illustrator, Palmer Cox, had, from the 1880s, popularised the Brownies in his books and poems published in the popular children's magazine *St Nicholas*. 'Brownies, like fairies and goblins, are imaginary little sprites, who are supposed to delight in harmless pranks and helpful deeds. They work and sport while weary households sleep, and never allow themselves to be seen by mortal eyes', said the introduction in each of his books of illustrated verse. The extreme popularity of the little Brownie characters made the name a natural one for Eastman to choose. In

The camera designer Frank Brownell

the early advertisements, the Brownie figures were illustrated with the camera, and a Brownie was shown on the carton in which the camera was sold. The similarity to Brownell's name seems to have been coincidental; his family confirm that Palmer Cox's characters were the source of inspiration. In Palmer Cox's publications after 1900, a little character carrying a box camera appears regularly in the drawings.

The first Brownie camera was made of jute board and wood, with a simple lens and rotary

shutter for time and instantaneous exposures. It sold for five shillings in Britain or one dollar in America. No viewfinder was fitted, but like the earlier Kodak cameras, the Brownie camera had V lines marked on the top, to assist with aiming. After July 1900, a clip-on reflecting viewfinder was available as an optional extra, price one shilling. On the first production model, the camera had a push-on box-lid back, which did not prove secure enough in use; within a month or so, the back had been altered to a hinged type, secured by a sliding latch. The Brownie camera took six pictures 2¼ inches square on a cartridge roll film; to reduce the cost further, rolls of paper negative film were available, selling in America at 10 cents, compared with 15 cents for the celluloid film. Developing, printing and mounting of the six-exposure films cost 40 cents. The Brownie camera was extensively advertised in the popular press, especially in children's magazines; significantly, the *St Nicholas* magazine for June 1900 carried a full-page advertisement for the new camera. Young purchasers were invited to join the Brownie Camera Club, and to enter its competitions; the 1902 competition in England attracted 10,000 entries.

Within a year, over 100,000 Brownie cameras had been sold, nearly half of them in England. In 1901 a new model was introduced, the No 2 Brownie camera, taking 2¼ by 3¼ inch pictures. Although it cost twice as much as the first model, it was of more elaborate construction, with two reflecting viewfinders, the rotary shutter and lens

Above *The Brownie camera was introduced in 1900; this example was made the following year*

Below *Early Brownie camera advertisements featured the little characters created by Palmer Cox*

Above *Like the first Kodak camera, the Brownie camera at first had no viewfinder; it was just directed at the subject*

Below *Butcher's Carbine camera* left *and Houghton's Bo 3 Ensign camera* right *are similar to the No 3 Folding Kodak camera* centre

Below right, far right *The time exposure feature on even simple cameras made indoor portraiture possible by natural or artificial light*

with a choice of three apertures on a sliding strip. The No 2 Brownie camera became the most popular of the roll film box cameras, and survived in one form or another until the late 1950s. The original camera was designated the No 1 Brownie camera and continued in production until 1915. Larger size Brownie box cameras followed — the No 2A (2½ by 4½ inches) in 1907 and the No 3 (3¼ by 4¼ inches) in 1908. The great success of the Brownie cameras soon encouraged other manufacturers to market models. In Britain, George Houghton and Sons introduced a similar camera, the No 1 Scout in 1901. Like the Brownie camera, the Scout had no viewfinder, but one was available as an optional extra; it took the same size roll film, with pictures 2¼ by 2¼ inches. In 1909 Houghtons produced several box cameras under the Ensign trade-mark, taking negatives from 2¼ inches square to 3¼ by 4¼ inches and of generally similar design to their Kodak counterparts. In the United States the Ansco company sold a similar range of cameras from 1906, under the name Buster Brown.

The very compact Folding Pocket Kodak camera of 1897 had been followed by two new models in 1899 — the 1A Folding Pocket Kodak camera (2½ by 4¼ inches) and the 2 Folding Pocket Kodak camera (3½ by 3½ inches). Soon, the

range was extended by three new sizes: No 3 (3¼ by 4¼ inches) in 1900, No 0 (1⅞ by 2½ inches) in 1902 and No 3A (3¼ by 5½ inches) in 1903. The No 3 Folding Pocket Kodak camera was very popular, especially in Britain, where about 100,000 were sold between 1900 and 1914. The No 3A Folding Pocket Kodak camera was also successful, taking a postcard-sized photograph; prints could be made on cards with pre-printed backs for posting. Folding cameras with even larger sizes were rather less popular; the No 4 Folding Kodak camera (4 by 5 inches) of 1907 and the No 4A Folding Kodak camera (4¼ by 6½ inches) of 1906 were among the largest of the daylight loading Kodak roll film cameras. Only 1,300 of the No 4A were sold in Britain. The folding principle was also extended to the Brownie camera range, with the No 2 Folding Brownie camera (2¼ by 3¼) in 1904, the No 3 (3¼ by 4¼) in 1905 and the No 3A (3¼ by 5½ inches) in 1909. The Folding Brownie cameras had less advanced specifications than their Kodak counterparts and a more economical finish. They were correspondingly less expensive — the No 3A Folding Brownie camera cost £2.10 in 1910, compared with £4.50 for the No 3A Folding Pocket Kodak camera. These Folding Brownie cameras were of a horizontal form, with the film running from side to side of the camera, a pattern which had been seen in a number of early European folding roll film cameras, such as the Lizar's Challenge (1898), Thornton-Pickard Automan (1901) and various Busch models such as the Cycam (1899) and the Tribees (1900) as well as the No 2 Folding Pocket Kodak camera. Other manufacturers adopted the upright arrangement of the later Folding Pocket Kodak cameras. Houghton's Ensign folding cameras were closely modelled on the Kodak equivalent; the first, the No 3 Ensign camera, was introduced in 1907, and used the same roll film as the No 3 Folding Pocket Kodak camera. W. Butcher's Carbine camera range, introduced in 1903, was also similar to the Kodak counterpart; in 1907, the Selfix Carbine incorporated a mechanism whereby lowering the baseboard of the camera automatically erected it for use. This principle, simplifying the operation of the camera, had appeared in two years before in improved models of the No 1 and No 1A Folding Pocket Kodak cameras.

The new generations of box and folding cameras had departed somewhat from the extreme simplicity of the original Kodak cameras. Most made some adjustment of exposure possible, by varying the lens aperture and, on the folding cameras, by altering the shutter speed. However,

25

The Quick Focus Kodak camera was adjusted instantaneously for a pre-set distance by touching a button

be sharply defined in the picture for a given setting of the lens aperture and focusing distance. The No 4 Screen Focus Kodak camera (1904) had an ingenious construction which permitted the light-tight film compartments to be swung up and away from the camera back so that a ground glass screen could be fitted for critical focusing when required, although the camera could be used as a normal snapshot camera. Similar construction was used in the Wizard Duplex camera (1904) and the French Universelle camera (1908). The strangest solution to the focusing problem was found in the No 3B Quick Focus Kodak camera (1906). When closed, the camera looked like a conventional box camera; on the side was a focusing scale which could be preset to a suitable distance. When a picture was to be taken, a button was pressed on the camera side, whereupon the front of the camera was pushed forward rapidly (and noisily) to an appropriate distance by internal springs!

An interesting, if specialised, snapshot camera from the first decade of this century was the Panoram Kodak camera. Made in two sizes, No 1 (1900) and No 4 (1899), the Panoram cameras were of box form, with a swivelling lens which rotated when the release was pressed, producing a panoramic picture on the roll film held on curved guides in the camera. The No 1 covered an angle of 112° in a picture of 2¼ by 7 inches, and the No 4 an angle of 142° in a picture of 3½ by 12 inches. Although designed for landscapes and groups, if held on its side, the Panoram Kodak camera could also be used to photograph mountains, towers and waterfalls. Although the principle of the rotating lens panoramic camera was not new (panoramic Daguerretotypes had been taken by this method in the 1840s), its application to the snapshot camera was novel. In 1903, the Eastman Kodak Company introduced an improved roll film. The earlier film, after processing, was very prone to roll up into a tight cylinder, as the gelatin coating contracted on drying. This made it very difficult to handle when printing. The new film was made non-curling by coating the back with a plain gelatin layer; the stresses of the two layers were thus equalised, and the film stayed flat. The new 'N.C.' film was also partly orthochromatic — that is to say, it was sensitive to some extent to green and yellow colours, giving an improved tonal rendering in the photograph. The earlier 'ordinary' films had been sensitive only to blue light, and thus rendered greens and reds as much darker in the picture than they would appear in life. An improvement to the backing paper of the Eastman roll films was made

for most snapshot photography, these settings could be ignored and the camera left set to a snapshot exposure of 1/25 second at around f/16. However, to enable the novice to make the most of his camera, an exposure calculation system was patented in 1908, appearing in commercial form in the 1908-9 catalogue of George Murphy Inc., the American photographic firm. The Autotime scales replaced the shutter speed and aperture scales of a range of popular shutters and lenses, being fixed by the same screws. Once fitted, it was necessary only to set the top or shutter scale to the prevailing light conditions, and the bottom or aperture scale to the subject type and the exposure would be correct. By eliminating the need to have to master the relationship between shutter speed and aperture, the Autotime scale was a great aid to the beginner. The Autotime scale was fitted to Kodak cameras from 1911. The box cameras were of fixed focus, the lens being set at a compromise position, with everything from six or seven feet away being adequately sharp in the negative. The folding cameras, especially those of large format, usually had some provision for adjusting the lens to film distance. To simplify the setting of the camera accurately and quickly, most of the folding Kodak cameras had movable catches which could be set at any desired distance on the focusing scale. The camera front was pulled out to the position of the catch and was then automatically focused at the correct distance. An alternative device was fitted to the Ensign Model E camera of 1902, using the patented Cornex depth of field indicator. This scale showed the amount of the subject that would

Eastman used the work of a number of leading American artists in his early advertising: top left *T. Perara, 1893;* top right *Frederic Remington, 1904;* left *G. Allan Gilbert, 1905;* above *Edward Penfield, 1905*

in 1909. The original black paper backing carried white letters, which were inclined to 'off-set' or transfer to the sensitive emulsion with which they were in contact when wound on the spool. The new 'duplex' paper was red, with black numbers on the side in contact with the emulsion, and black on the other. This disposed of the 'off-setting' problem, and has remained the pattern for roll film backing papers to the present day.

The great reductions in cost and complication of photography brought many hundreds of thousands of newcomers to photography. In 1902

The first Panoram Kodak camera was introduced in 1899. The swivelling lens recorded a panoramic view of up to 142 degrees on the roll film running on curved guides inside the camera

The Daily Mail reported 'the demand for snapshot cameras has this year beaten all records. No doubt the Coronation celebrations were responsible for a good deal of the liberal buying that has been indulged in, but . . . it would appear as if the photographic "craze" . . . is likely to continue!' Although from the earliest days of photography women had followed it as both amateurs and professionals, nevertheless until this century it had been predominately a male pursuit. The new snapshot cameras, light, simple and inexpensive, and the developing and printing services support-ing them, attracted large numbers of women to take up photography. On a day's visit for competi-tive photography to London's Wembley Park in 1903, over a third of the participants were women. *The Photographic News* in September 1905 reported from a Birmingham newspaper:

> Thousands of Birmingham girls are scattered about the holiday resorts of Britain this month, and a very large percentage of them are armed with cameras, mainly, of course, of the hand variety. The girls snapshot their sweethearts, the young married women take their young hopefuls, and the old married women, and the old men, too, submit to be posed by the youthful enthusiast . . . there are two points of marked interest in connection with the camera this year. Firstly, the ladies have taken to buying and using cameras themselves . . . It is as much a feminine as a masculine hobby nowadays — perhaps more so. And, secondly, more amateurs have taken to developing and finishing their own pictures'.

This latter possibility had been made much more practical by the introduction in 1902 of the Kodak Film Tank and of the improved version, the Kodak Tank Developer in 1905. These machines allowed the photographer to develop roll films in daylight; no darkroom of any sort was needed.

Walking advertisements for the Kodak Exhibition and lectures by Dr Dixon, 1904

The processed negatives could be printed in daylight, using printing out paper such as the Kodak Solio paper or the Ilford P.O.P. Although the vast majority of snapshot photographers continued to send their films for trade processing, the attraction of the speed and economy of do-it-yourself processing was considerable.

To promote snapshot photography in England, a new magazine was introduced in December 1905. Called *The Kodak Recorder*, it was published as a quarterly until 1913. Like its predecessor, *The Kodak News*, the *Recorder* carried articles on technical matters, picture-taking techniques and new products. The second issue, of March 1906, carried a report on the photographic activities of Queen Alexandra who, it said, 'has been a keen amateur photographer for the last fifteen years'. The Queen's favourite camera was a No 4 Bulls-Eye Special Kodak camera; in 1902, she granted George Eastman a Royal Warrant as purveyor of photographic materials to the Royal family. In 1908, over 140 of her snapshots were published in *Queen Alexandra's Christmas Gift Book*, published by the *Daily Telegraph* and sold for charity. Many hundreds of thousands of copies were sold, the informal snapshots from Her Majesty's camera giving a view of the Royal Family quite unlike anything seen before by the general public. Some of the Queen's pictures were included in a travelling exhibition which toured the British Isles in 1904 and 1905. Kodak Ltd engaged a popular lecturer, Dr Dixon, to travel with the exhibition and to talk on aspects of photography. The tours were enormously successful; Dr Dixon talked to packed houses everywhere he went. The *Bournemouth Daily Echo* reported 'at Croydon . . . the doors had to be locked, so great was the crush, while at St Leonards the great hall, capable of seating 1,500 people, was found too small, and people had to be turned away from the doors'. The *Amateur Photographer* said: 'The Kodak Travelling Exhibition seems to be stirring up the country like a revolutionary banner as it passes from town to town . . . creating a yearning for camera and lens in others in who heretofore the wish was dormant'. In the autumn of 1905, the show went to the United States, for a highly successful tour in towns through the country. Popular photography had arrived, and became established as a pastime throughout society by the end of the first decade of this century.

4 The soldier's camera

Although the first of the cartridge loading cameras, the Pocket Kodak camera, had taken pictures of small format, 1½ by 2 inches, the majority of popular cameras produced negatives of much larger size. Then in 1912 the Eastman Kodak Company produced what became the most popular camera of its age. Called the Vest Pocket Kodak camera, like the earlier No 0 Folding Pocket Kodak camera it took negatives 1⅞ by 2½ inches, but by using a more compact all-metal spool and metal body the size of the camera was greatly reduced. When closed the camera was small, measuring only 1 inch by 2⅜ by 4¾ inches; it was erected by pulling out the front on lazy-tong struts. It was immediately successful; by the time that this model was finally discontinued, in 1926, almost two million had been sold. Although the Vest Pocket Kodak camera was by far the most popular camera of its type, it was not the first small folding roll film camera. An English company, Houghtons Ltd, had introduced in 1909 a small collapsible camera called the Ensignette. The first model took pictures 2¼ by 1½ inches in size and measured, when closed, only 4 by 2 by ¾ inches.

Houghton's Ensignette camera, 1909 left *and the Vest Pocket Kodak camera, 1912* right, *two very popular pocket-sized roll film cameras*

Two prints from negatives made in Autographic cameras, with data written below each picture

In 1912 a second size was introduced for 2 by 3 inch negatives. Although the Ensignette never attained the tremendous popularity of the Vest Pocket Kodak camera, it nonetheless sold very well, becoming one of the few cameras by another manufacturer for which the Kodak company manufactured special roll films. The new small formats were extended to the box camera with the No 0 Brownie camera (1914) which took the vest pocket size film. At the other extreme of size, a new large box camera, the No 2C Brownie camera, was marketed in 1917, taking pictures 2⅞ by 4⅞ inches in size. Other manufacturers produced and sold box and folding roll film cameras in the 1910s; in the United States, the Seneca Scout camera and the Sears Roebuck Kewpie cameras did well, together with the popular Ansco Buster Brown range. In England, the Ensign box and folding cameras, made in four sizes by Houghtons Ltd, maintained their popularity.

A major technical innovation of the decade was based upon patents granted to Henry J. Gaisman. Gaisman proposed a roll film in which a form of carbon paper was carried between the film and the backing paper. Pressure with a metal stylus on the backing caused the carbon paper to become transparent at that point and light penetrating the backing paper could thus expose the film. George Eastman paid Gaisman the then enormous sum of $300,000 for the rights to the patents on the film and the cameras in which it could be used. The Folding Pocket Kodak camera range was redesigned and the new Autographic Kodak cameras were launched in 1914 in four sizes: No 1 Junior, 1A, 3 and 3A. A No 2C Junior followed in 1916. In 1915, the Autographic feature was added to the Vest Pocket Kodak cameras, and to a redesigned range of Folding Brownie cameras. The operation of the Autographic cameras was simple.

'Touch a spring and a little door opens in the back . . . write with pencil or stylus on the red paper of the Autographic Film Cartridge; expose from 2 to 5 seconds; close door. When your negatives are developed a permanent photographic reproduction of the writing will appear on the intersections

31

The Autographic Kodak cameras were introduced in 1914. By 'writing' with a stylus on the backing paper of the film, exposed by lifting a flap, information could be printed onto the film. The lower illustration is of an Autographic film showing the pressure-sensitive tissue between the film and the backing paper

between the negatives . . . By turning the winding key slightly and advancing the paper the width of the slot you can have the writing appear on the picture itself. Any picture that is worth taking is worth a date or title. The places of interest you visit, the autographs of friends you photograph, interesting facts about the children, their age at the time the picture was made — all these things add to the value of a picture'.

The Autographic feature was on all popular Kodak cameras (except the Brownie box cameras) until the early 1930s. Users of the earlier Folding Pocket Kodak cameras could make use of the new Autographic film by buying a modified back to replace the original.

An interesting innovation was incorporated in Special models of the No 3A Autographic Kodak camera (1916) and the No 1A Autographic Kodak camera (1917). A rangefinding system was directly coupled to the focusing mechanism. The subject to be photographed was viewed in a small optical unit, placed below the lens, in which the scene was divided into three strips. By adjusting

Below *The No 3A Autographic Kodak Special camera of 1916 was the first to incorporate a coupled rangefinder to ensure accurate focusing. The optical unit can be seen below the lens*

Above *The Kodak Girl in her distinctive striped dress was introduced into Kodak Limited advertising in 1910. This drawing is by Fred Pegram, a popular cartoonist and regular contributor to* Punch, *who created many Kodak advertisements*

the focusing mechanism, the view in the centre strip could be moved until it matched that of the two outer strips. When the horizontal lines of the subject appeared unbroken across all three strips, the camera was correctly focused. This was the first appearance of a feature which was to be incorporated in many expensive cameras in the 1930s and 1940s.

The introduction of the Vest Pocket Kodak camera, with yet another roll film size, led the Eastman Kodak Company to develop a classification of film sizes. Up to this time, films had been identified by the type of camera they fitted and given such designations as 3FPK, 2 Bull's-Eye. The new system used a consecutive series of

33

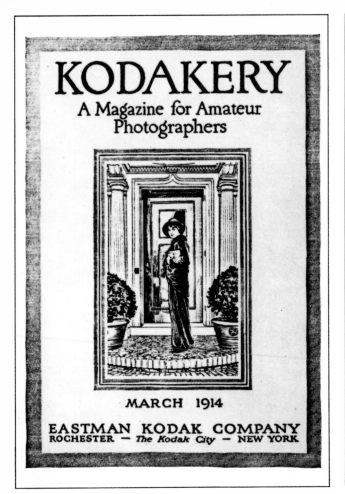

The first issue of the magazine Kodakery *appeared in the United States in March 1914*

Kodak in Camp

From reveille to taps, each hour will bring something new into the life of every young soldier. New surroundings, new habits, new faces, and new friendships will make for him a new world—a world full of interest to him *to-day* and and a world upon which he will often dwell in memory when peace has come again.

And this new world of his offers Kodak opportunities that will relieve the tedium of camp routine at the time and will afterward provide what will be to him and his friends the most interesting of all books—his Kodak album.

In 1917 American soldiers were encouraged to use photography to record their new experiences

numbers, allocated to the various film sizes in the order in which they had been introduced. Thus film for the first cartridge loading camera, the No 2 Bullet camera, became No 101, that for the Pocket Kodak camera, No 102, the film for the No 4 Bullet camera, No 103 and so on. The new Vest Pocket film was numbered 127. (A full list of the sizes is given in the appendix.)

When war broke out in Europe in 1914, there was a boom in photographic business, reaching a peak in 1917. Families bought cameras to photograph loved oes leaving England, perhaps never to return. Soldiers bought cameras to take with them, despite the fact that possession of a camera while on active service in the front line was a court martial offence — carrying a death penalty in certain circumstances. By far the most popular camera with the soldier was the Vest Pocket Kodak camera, small enough to be carried (and concealed). It was advertised as The Soldier's Kodak camera, the owner being encouraged to 'Make your own picture record of the War'. A

'military' case in pigskin, by which the camera could be carried attached to the belt, was sold. Sales of the Vest Pocket Kodak camera in Great Britain in 1915 were five times those of the previous year. When America entered the war in 1917, the Vest Pocket Kodak camera was as popular with the doughboy as it was with his European counterpart. American soldiers were allowed free use of cameras in camp or overseas, although they were not allowed to take them into the trenches.

In 1910 an important new motif was introduced to Kodak Ltd's poster and magazine advertising. From the days of the first Kodak camera the company had used figures of girls with cameras in its advertising and from 1901 a consistent use was made of photographs of 'The Kodak Girl' and her camera in advertising in both America and England. In a 1910 poster, drawn for Kodak Ltd by the leading poster artist John Hassell, the Kodak Girl was drawn in a long striped dress and the same figure was incorporated in full page magazine advertisements. For the next thirty or more years, the Kodak Girl in her distinctive striped dress formed the central motif of Kodak Ltd's advertising. Among the leading artists commissioned to design Kodak Girl advertisements were Claude A. Shepperson, Horace Rich, Dudley Harvey and Fred Pegram — the latter producing the greater proportion of Kodak advertisements in the years between the two World Wars. The Kodak Girl proved very popular with the public; her striped dress, it is said, had a strong influence on popular fashion; certainly, no fancy dress competition was complete without a Kodak Girl entrant. In the advertisements, the Kodak Girl, always with her folding camera, was shown in a wide variety of settings, ranging from the English countryside to more exotic locations in Africa and the Far East. Her message was simple and direct — 'No holiday is complete without a Kodak camera'. Although a similar figure was used in a 1912 advertising campaign in America, no such consistent use of the Kodak Girl in a striped dress was made by the Eastman Kodak Company. They, too, had used the best artists to design their early advertisements, including Frederic Remington, Charles Allen Gilbert, Ed Penfield and A. B. Frost. After 1910, however, they tended to use photographs rather than

On this page, three snapshots from the First World War. Below *'The Early Morning Cup of Tea', 1918*

Top Royal Flying Corps officer meets local children, 1915

Above Bizarre group in gasmasks, 1917

drawings as the basis for advertisements. In England, the Kodak company had promoted snapshot photography through its magazines *Kodak News* and *The Kodak Recorder;* no comparable publications were produced in the United States, where more direct advertising was relied on. Then in March 1914 the Eastman Kodak Company launched a new publication, *Kodakery*, available by subscription through photographic dealers. Like its English predecessors, *Kodakery* dispensed advice and product news and illustrated the work of amateur photographers. A year's free subscription was given with each new camera sale; by 1920 there were over 5,000 paying subscribers, in addition to the many thousands of new customers. *Kodakery* was published until June 1932.

5 Colourful cameras

After the First World War there was a boom in photographic sales. In 1920, five times as many cameras were sold as in 1914; film sales increased in the same proportion. Snapshot photography had become an accepted feature of life for many families, as apparatus and materials became cheaper. Wage rates had risen steeply after the War, but prices of photographic goods had not increased in the same proportion. In 1910, the cost of a No 2 Brownie camera was about 35% of the average weekly wage of a Kodak factory worker; in 1920 the proportion was only 20%. In the first few years of the 1920s there were no major developments in snapshot photography. In the aftermath of the War, a number of European companies went to the wall, or survived only through mergers. In England, Houghton's Ltd and W. Butcher and Sons, who had merged their manufacturing facilities in 1915, joined forces fully in 1926. In 1921, a consortium of English firms, Paget, Rajar, Marion, Kershaw and Rotary Photographic, was formed under the trade name APeM, and began manufacturing a range of products including simple cameras. In Germany, Zeiss Ikon Ges. was formed in 1926 by an amalgamation of Zeiss, Ica, Goerz, Ernemann and Contessa-Nettel. In the United States, the Ansco company combined with the American Agfa organisation in 1928.

Rising labour costs accelerated the move from the use of wood to metal in camera manufacture. Wood had to be individually worked; metal could be pressed or stamped and easily mass produced. From 1924 the popular No 2 and 2A Brownie box cameras were made from aluminium instead of wood and card. By the end of the 1920s virtually all mass produced cameras were made from metal

The Kodak Girl on a giant camera in an advertising pageant, 1921

or moulded from such plastic materials as Bakelite. One of the first moulded cameras to be mass produced in England was made by the APeM group in 1928, under the name Rajar No 6. It was a large, rather clumsy collapsible camera, and was distributed largely through premium sales schemes. These became increasingly popular in the 1920s; cigarette and soap manufacturers, magazines, chocolate makers and others provided coupons which if collected brought the customer a free camera, or one at a big discount. Many homes acquired their first camera by courtesy of Black Cat cigarettes, Cadbury's chocolates or Wright's Coal Tar Soap.

Most box cameras, with lenses of fixed focus, permitted photography only at distances of six or seven feet and beyond; head and shoulder close-up photographs were not practical without a portrait attachment, a complication for many people. In 1927 the Houghton-Butcher company in England introduced the Ensign All-Distance camera, in which a simple adjustment could set the lens for head and shoulder portraits as well as distant views and groups. The All-Distance Ensign camera incorporated a wire frame eye level viewfinder, in addition to the two conventional small reflecting finders which were a standard fitting on virtually all box cameras. Eye level frame finders had been fitted to some folding cameras, such as the Busch Pockam camera of 1902 and the Agfa Standard camera of 1926, but on a box camera the idea was unusual. The new Kodak Ltd camera factory at Harrow responded in 1929 with a range of No 2 Portrait Brownie cameras, in which a portrait lens for close-ups could be brought into position by pressing a lever. Until the late 1920s, all Kodak cameras had been manufactured in Rochester, USA or Toronto, Canada. In 1927 Kodak Ltd acquired the New Zealand Pavilion from the British Empire Exhibition, held at Wembley in 1924-5; it was moved, in sections, to the Harrow factory and reassembled. The No 2 Portrait Brownie camera was one of the first products from the new plant, much of the machinery of which had been brought over from the Toronto factory.

The Kodak Girl also featured in life-sized cut-outs for shop displays in the 1920s and 1930s

In addition to Fred Pegram below, below right *A. Wallis Mills* centre right *and Claude Shepperson* far right *were among the many well known illustrators who produced Kodak Girl advertisements*

Top *The Vanity Kodak camera of 1928 produced in a range of six colours with matching cases*

Centre *The Ensign 'All-Distance' box camera range, introduced in 1927, had a pull-out lens mount, permitting close-ups to be taken. The No 2 Portrait Brownie camera* right *had a built-in close-up lens, came in seven colours and was made at the Kodak factory in Harrow, Middlesex, in 1929*

Above *The original design for the Kodak Fellowship badge* left; *later the badge was altered* right

To attract the feminine photographer a dramatically different range of cameras appeared at the end of the 1920s. In 1928 the Eastman Kodak Company introduced a new range of Vest Pocket Kodak cameras, Series III, in five colour schemes: Bluebird (deep blue), Cockatoo (green), Jenny Wren (brown), Redbreast (red) and Sea Gull (gray). Called the Vanity Kodak cameras, they were supplied in a matching case, lined with coloured silk. All parts, both metal and leather, were coloured and embossed gold lines were used as embellishment. The cameras were styled by the leading American designer Walter Dorwin Teague, who also designed the case. In the same year, the Vanity Kodak Ensemble appeared — a coloured case containing a coloured Vest Pocket Kodak camera model B, with a matching lipstick holder, compact, mirror and change pocket. The Ansco company also in 1928, sold a similar Vanity outfit containing a built-in box camera. The humble Brownie box cameras appeared in a range of six colours, as well as the traditional black, in 1929. In that year, the Ensign box and folding cameras were available in three colour schemes. Attractive though they appeared, the coloured cameras were not altogether successful. As with any fashion item, tastes changed; some colours were more popular than others, leaving hard-to-move stock on the dealer's shelves. Colour cameras had to match the outfit of the lady they were meant to attract; if it did not, it might be left at home. By 1934, popular cameras had reverted for the most part to the traditional black colour.

The Kodak Girl continued as the theme of Kodak advertising in England in the 1920s, Fred Pegram supplying many of the designs. Full size cut-out figures of the Kodak Girl were supplied to dealers for display, and live Kodak Girls attended fêtes, pageants and processions. In January 1923 Kodak Ltd published the first issue of *The Kodak Magazine,* which, like its American predecessor *Kodakery* aimed to help non-specialist photographers to get the most from their cameras. In January 1925 the editor wrote:

'Often when you have noticed another Kodak enthusiast picture-making you must have wondered what exposure and stop he was using, and wished you could ask him for help — or, possibly, give him advice! — but you "did not know him". It has been suggested that "Kodak Magazine" badges should be provided, to fix to cameras or camera cases, to enable fellow readers to recognise one another'.

The response to this suggestion was tremendous; in June the editor announced the formation of The

Kodak Fellowship, open to all readers, who were invited to send sixpence for a lapel badge or brooch. The Fellowship was extraordinarily successful; within a year local groups were arranging rambles and lectures, competitions and exhibitions. The Fellowship badge, as the editor had hoped, really was the 'means of founding very many delightful friendships, on the ground of common interests'. The Fellowship, under the guidance of its secretary, Mr C. L. Clarke, continued to flourish until the outbreak of War in 1939 put an end to it, and to *The Kodak Magazine*.

A measure of the hold which photography had gained upon the popular imagination may be judged from the trade, which grew and flourished during the 1920s and 1930s, in small souvenirs and other items styled to look like cameras. They appeared in amazing diversity. Equally amazing, even bizarre, ingenuity was applied to the selection of objects thought to be suitable for such stylistic treatment. Small china place souvenirs — 'A Present from Margate' — were shaped to resemble snapshot cameras, perhaps a logical extension of the long tradition of furnishing such products for a souvenir hungry public. Much odder were the camera-styled biscuit tins, portable gramophones, powder compacts and cigarette cases. The snapshot camera had achieved such a desirable status in the public's eye that it provided a selling point even when its form was impressed, occasionally with disastrous results, upon objects normally with their own distinctive shape.

Above *A shop display card for Wellington roll films, with a cartoon by W. Heath Robinson. Note the number of cameras concealed in the scene*

Below *Articles drawing on the snapshot camera for their stylistic inspiration:* left *compact, lipstick holder and cigarette case in the form of a small folding camera;* centre *Thorens' portable gramophone in the form of a large folding camera;* right *china souvenirs in the form of cameras*

6 Smaller cameras and faster films

Despite the depression years, the 1930s saw a huge increase in the popularity of photography. By 1930 the cost of the No 2 Brownie camera represented only 15% of the average weekly wage of the Kodak factory worker. Film prices fell too; in 1930 the price of a roll of film for a conventional box camera was reduced to one shilling from one shilling and twopence, and the number of exposures was increased from six to eight. Such film manufacturers as Agfa and Lumière introduced simple cameras for the mass market, as did leading camera makers such as Voigtlander and Zeiss-Ikon. The decade started with an extraordinary

The Anniversary Hawkeye camera, 1930. More than half a million of these special Kodak cameras were given away by George Eastman

event in America. To celebrate the fiftieth anniversary of the founding of his company, George Eastman announced that he would give a box camera to any child whose twelfth birthday fell in 1930. The cameras were special versions of the No 2 Hawkeye camera Model C, a simple box type normally sold for $1.25. The Anniversary Hawkeye cameras were covered with a light brown leatherette with gilt trimmings and carried a gilt anniversary badge. In all, 500,000 were distributed in America, and a further 50,000 in Canada. The cameras were sent out through dealers in May 1930; all were gone in two or three days.

The artist and designer Walter Dorwin Teague had advised Eastman on the styling and colour schemes of the range of coloured Kodak cameras in the late 1920s. In 1930 he designed two new box cameras, the Nos 2 and 2A Beau Brownie cameras. By using a doublet lens — one with a lens in front of the shutter as well as behind — the cameras could be made shorter in length. Teague created a striking two-toned geometric pattern to decorate the front panel; the two cameras were available in tan, rose, green, black or blue colours, with leatherette matching the enamelled panel. A similar styling was used to embellish the No 1A Gift Kodak camera sold in the same year; a cedarwood presentation box with a matching enamelled motif on the lid was supplied with it. These elegant cameras were the last of the coloured range; subsequent models reverted to the traditional black finish. Teague's next camera for the Eastman Kodak Company was the Baby Brownie camera (1934). A small camera, using the 127 'vest pocket' roll film, it was moulded in black plastic material, enabling the cost to be brought

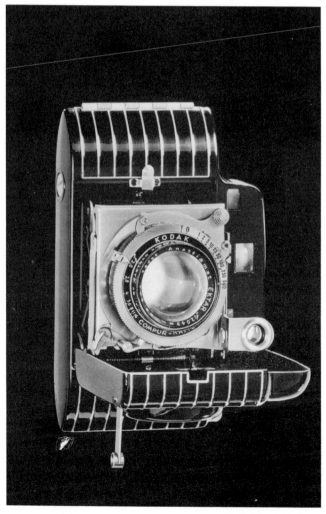

Some of the cameras styled by Walter Dorwin Teague, an eminent American industrial designer responsible for an enormous amount of work throughout the 1930s. Top the 2 and 2A Beau Brownie cameras, 1930; left the Kodak Bantam Special camera, 1936 and above the Baby Brownie camera, 1934

Above *A group of 1930s cameras in moulded plastic:* top left
No 2 Hawkette camera, 1930; top centre *Rajar No 6 camera,
1928;* top right *Ebner camera, 1933;* bottom left *Kodak
Bantam f8/camera, 1936;* bottom right *Coronet Vogue
camera, 1936*

Below *A Kodak poster design by Arthur Ferrier, another very
popular illustrator whose drawings of attractive girls were a
speciality. The changing style of the illustrations emphasises the
durability of the Kodak girl symbol.*

down once again to one dollar, the price of the
original Brownie camera of 1900. Teague also
styled the Jiffy Kodak VP camera and the Kodak
Bantam cameras introduced the following year,
but his masterpiece was the Kodak Bantam
Special camera of 1936. A precision-built miniature camera for the newly introduced 828 roll film,
it was beautifully styled in black enamel with
raised bright lines of polished metal.

Two new roll films appeared in 1932. Identical
in width and picture size to the 120 and 116 roll
films, the new 620 and 616 films were carried on
slimmer all metal spools, making possible an
appreciable reduction in the size of the folding
camera. A new range of Six-20 Kodak cameras
was introduced to take the new films, and Six-20
Brownie box cameras were designed to accept
them. The growing popularity among photographic enthusiasts of the miniature cameras such
as the Leica and Contax soon had its effect on the
design of cameras for the mass market. Improvements in negative materials and the wider availa-
bility of enlarging services from photofinishers
made the use of small negative sizes more
practical. One way of achieving smaller picture
sizes was to double the number of exposures on the
conventional roll film. Thus, the Baby Box Tengor
and the Kolibri cameras of 1930, and the Baby

Ikonta and Nagel Ranca cameras of 1931 took sixteen pictures 4.5 by 3 cm on standard 127 roll film. Others, like the Soho Tuon (1934), Ebner folding (1934) and Dallmeyer Dual (1931) took sixteen pictures 4.5 by 6 cm on 120 roll film. Some cameras were made to take two formats, adjustable by inserting a mask in the film plane. Examples include the Coronet Every Distance (1936) and Ensign E-20 (1937) box cameras, and the Voigtlander Inos (1931), Certo Super Sport (1935) and Selfix-220 (1937) folding cameras. Some cameras made use of smaller, new roll films; the 828 Kodak Bantam film, for 2.8 by 4 cm pictures, has already been mentioned. Other cameras, such as the all plastic Univex camera (1933) and the Coronet Midget (1934), were little more than toys, but the Ensign Midget folding camera, derived from the popular Ensignette camera in 1934, was capable of good results. These miniature pocketable cameras started a trend which continued in the postwar years and which led to today's highly popular pocket cameras.

Plastics moulding techniques developed rapidly in the 1930s, and many cameras were mass produced using this method. Some, such as the Kodak Bantam and Jiffy V.P. cameras, have been mentioned already; others include the Coronet Vogue (1936) and Soho Cadet (1931) folding cameras and the elegantly designed Ebner folding

Above *The Ensign E20 dual format box camera, for eight or sixteen exposures on 120 roll film*

Below *Some miniature snapshot cameras, made practical by improved film materials in the 1930s:* left *Baby Box Tengor, 1930;* centre *Ensign Midget, 1934;* right *Univex camera, 1933*

*The new fully orthochromatic roll films of the 1930s, especially
when used with a yellow filter, gave greatly improved renderings
of skies* below *compared with the earlier 'ordinary' films* above

44

camera, in which the rather clumsy appearance of many of the early plastic cameras, such as the Kodak No 2 Hawkette camera (1930), was replaced by a smoothly streamlined shape. The manufacture of glass lenses, even the simple ones used in box cameras, was a lengthy and thus relatively expensive process. The English experimental engineer Arthur Kingston patented in 1934 the first effective plastic lens moulding system to give repeatable results for precision lens making. Kingston used the new acrylic plastics materials to make spectacle and opera glass lenses and viewfinder components for cameras. Although he designed an ingenious all-plastics camera incorporating his plastic lenses in 1936, it never passed beyond the prototype stage; the use of plastic lenses for cameras developed only in the post-war years.

The 1930s saw several important technical innovations which developed greatly in importance after the Second World War. The concept of the automatic control of exposure in the camera was the subject of many patents in this period. The first camera to incorporate this principle was the Super Kodak Six-20 camera of 1938. It was a folding camera of very advanced design, styled by Teague, with a photoelectric cell which set the lens aperture automatically as the shutter release was pressed. Although its $225 price made it a camera for the rich enthusiast only, it pioneered techniques which were to be applied to cameras for the mass market in the 1960s. The flashbulb was another development of the 1930s which was, in time, to influence the design of cameras for the popular market. At first, like the earlier magnesium flash powder devices, the flash bulb was fired after the camera shutter had been opened by hand. Thus, even simple box cameras could be used, provided they were placed on a solid support and had provision for time exposures. By the late 1930s, professional photographers had developed gadgets permitting the firing of the flash bulb to be synchronised to the opening of the shutter and camera manufacturers began to build-in synchronising devices. The first mass produced camera to incorporate flash synchronisation was the Falcon Press Flash in 1939. Other early flash cameras were the Agfa Shur-Flash and the Kodak Six-20 Flash Brownie box cameras, both of 1940. In post-war years, this feature was to become standard for all popular cameras. An alternative source of light for photography in the home was the Photoflood lamp, a high intensity electric light

The Super Kodak Six-20 camera (1938), another of Walter Dorwin Teague's attractive designs, and the first camera to have a fully automatic exposure control system

bulb which could be used in place of ordinary bulbs, permitting even box cameras to take interior photographs with relatively short exposures.

Along with the changes in camera design, improvements were made in the sensitive materials they used. In 1930 the German film manufacturing companies Hauff and Agfa introduced new roll films under the names Ultra and Isochrom respectively; the following year Kodak Verichrome film and Ilford Selochrome film appeared. These new materials were more sensitive than the ordinary film, had a wider latitude, tolerating considerable overexposure and had dye coatings on the back to reduce halation — the spread of light, or flare, around the bright parts of the picture. In particular, these new films were fully orthochromatic — that is to say, they responded equally to blue, green and yellow colours, although they were still not sensitive to red light. These improvements gave better tonal rendering in the picture and increased the scope of the simple camera. To exploit the better rendering of coloured objects, some cameras were introduced incorporating yellow filters which could be used to improve the reproduction of skies by increasing the contrast between blue sky and white clouds, which on the older films were virtually impossible to distinguish. The Agfa-Ansco No 2 Model G box camera of 1933, the Ensign All-Distance '20' camera of 1936 and the Agfa Billy-Clack camera of the same year are examples of cameras of this period incorporating filters. The higher sensitivity of the new films increased the risk that light would fog the film through the red window through which the film was observed when winding on and sliding or hinged covers began to be fitted. For the same reason, the new materials made the Autographic system impractical and the films were discontinued after 1934. Panchromatic roll films, sensitive to all colours, were also available in the 1930s. Ilford Pan roll film was sold from 1929; the high speed Kodak Super Sensitive Pan film was introduced in 1933. The higher speed panchromatic films were not suitable for simple non-adjustable cameras in normal conditions, but could be used in poor light — indoors or in the winter — when the ordinary films would have been useless. Used in adjustable cameras, with lenses of greater light-gathering capacity than the ordinary box camera, the new films greatly extended the scope of photography. While colour snapshot photography was essentially a post-war development, the first of the modern colour processes, Kodachrome film, was introduced in 1935. At first available only as a cine film for 16mm and 8mm cameras, the following year Kodachrome film was available for 35mm and 828 roll film cameras. In the same year, the first Agfacolor film was introduced, also in 35mm size. These processes, and others derived from them, are now almost universally used for popular photography.

When war broke out in Europe, a half-century after the beginning of popular photography, snapshot photography was an integral part of the life of most families. The real cost of a five shilling camera in 1939, allowing for inflation, was almost one hundredth of that of the first Kodak camera in 1888, bringing it within the reach of virtually every home. In the postwar years the major technical innovations of the 1930s — automatic exposure, miniaturisation, colour processes and flash — were developed and extended. To these were added the important new principles of drop-in cartridge loading and instant picture cameras — but that is another story!

A dive, effectively caught by the snapshot camera, 1910

People

People, from infancy to old age, have always formed the principal subject of the snapshot; the desire to have likenesses of family and friends has motivated most camera purchases. The snapshot documents the toys and games of childhood; it shows costume, sometimes formal, but usually very informal, the wearers coming from all walks of life. Something of the real character of the subject can be revealed in the snapshot, in a way that is rare in the professional portrait. Snapshots of children provide the greatest contrast with the studio portrait. Relaxed, at home with their toys, in everyday clothes, they show little or none of the restraint apparent in the professional portrait photograph.

Above left *1897 Period Piece*

Far left *Although snapshot cameras were relatively rare in 1891, the date this picture was taken, this little girl shows a remarkably developed awareness of being photographed*

Left *From its very early days, the snapshot camera was used to record everyday subject matter, such as this 1891 group of small-town youngsters*

Above *Three diverse companions and reluctant cat pose for this 1910 picture*

Top right *An 1892 'snapshot-time-exposure'. The little girl is holding what appears to be a 'Brownie' doll*

Above right *A remarkably impressive 1905 composition, strengthened by the low, waist-level viewpoint of the simple camera*

Above *A beautiful 1900 interior. The cane chair, screen and wallpaper reveal a taste for the 'aesthetic'*

Above right *HRH Princess Charles of Denmark – an 1897 snapshot by Princess Victoria of Wales*

Right *Mary, Duchess of Bedford, photographed in 1901 by a friend*

Far right *Winter 1910 and High Fashion*

Right *By 1904 this doll had seen better days, yet it remained an object of care and affection*

Below *The dresses and dining chairs underline the essentially middle-class ambience of this 1914 tea party*

Centre right *An aspiring general of 1912 deploys his forces*

Far right *A 1906 snapshot, redolent of the prosperity of a German family*

Below right *A young motor mechanic investigates the workings of his wonderfully in-period 1910 vehicle*

53

54

Above left *In 1901 commonplace street games such as leapfrog were rarely recorded. Snapshots such as this have left us with a significant record of how things were*

Far left *Edwardian London was more tolerant of nude bathing in its public places than today's 'permissive' society. Trafalgar Square, 1912*

Above *The street game again. Could today's mechanised distractions elicit such rapt concentration?*

Left *The gardener's son? Or a member of the household 'dressed-down' for the camera?*

Above left *A splendid family turnout for Coronation Day, 1902*

Above *Children's outing, 1918*

Above left *Family group on typical front doorstep. Note the characteristic close planting of shrubs, so popular in the Victorian and Edwardian suburbs in their heyday*

Far left *An example of the comic set-piece snapshot dating from 1912*

Above left *An idyll of the summer of 1916*

Above *The corridor of the railway carriage provides an unusual setting for this informal 1920 portrait*

Left *'A peaceful hour' with a pipe and a book, 1912*

Above left *Packing case and old pram wheels create a 1924 vehicle capable of providing endless enjoyment*

Far left *An early mobile ice-cream vendor, circa 1920, with minimal equipment*

Above *Another example, this time in 1932, of the dying art of do-it-yourself transport*

Left *A 1935 snapshot which effectively captures all the youthful pleasures of train watching*

Above left *Mrs George Bernard Shaw, photographed by Shaw himself in 1912*

Above *Posting a letter, 1927*

Above right *Middle-class family group, vintage 1914*

Right *The pedal-car changes its style. Compare this 1935 picture – the car was probably built two or three years earlier – with that at the bottom of page 53*

*'Mangling' – a childhood chore largely eliminated by the advent
of the washing machine*

Leisure

The snapshot camera had, from its inception, an important role as an adjunct to leisure activities. It soon became a desirable, even indispensable, accessory to take to picnics, on outings and motoring trips and to sporting events. Informal family pictures record the advent of radio, and the popularity of the gramophone. The street entertainer, once a feature of town life, and now almost extinct, was recorded in the snapshot for posterity. Hobbies, like painting or the activities of the keen amateur photographer, were sometimes documented by snapshooting relatives.

Above left *Steam-driven merry-go-round at a typical funfair, 1912*

Far left *A rather unusual picture of girls dancing in the street to the accompaniment of a barrel-organ*

Above *As late as 1903 the age-old entertainment of the dancing bear was still to be seen*

Left *The organ-grinder and his monkey, always popular with the children, 1920*

Above 'H.C. mending a puncture, Isle of Wight, August 1907'

Right Cycling, 1903 – the great Edwardian leisure activity

Above right A middle-class picnic of 1918

Far right In comparison, the Duke of Bedford and friends picnicking in 1902. Photographed by Mary, Duchess of Bedford

Above *Off for a holiday at a country station in 1910*

Right *'The Shoot', 1902*

Above right *A bizarre 1910 photo of triumphant mountaineers drinking a champagne toast in the middle of a snowstorm*

Far right *Some of the determination which governed the British Empire here applied to the field of play. 1912*

Top *An early motor-tricycle with its proud owners, 1902*

Above *'Aunt Madge and trailer, September 1901'*

Top centre *An amateur Toulouse-Lautrec of 1905. The illusion is spoiled only by the painting on the easel*

Top right *Augustus John, photographed in 1912 by his sitter, George Bernard Shaw*

Right *'An eminently suitable pastime for Gentlewomen'. 1912*

Top *A solitary photographic expert tackling things the hard way*

Above *Contrast the snapshooter and the 'serious' amateur photographer in this exotic location. 1905*

Above right *A camera club outing. This site today would be less conducive to such leisurely and methodical photographic procedures*

Right *Pets form an ever-popular subject for young camera owners*

Top *Brooklands Racetrack in its heyday – 1930*

Above *The school sports – the more versatile folding cameras available by 1930 made action snapshots a practical reality*

Right *An example of the informal moment – placing bets at the racetrack, 1936*

Far right *The snapshot camera was a natural adjunct to the hiking craze of the early 1930s*

Above, above right *The hiking craze produced candid snapshots by the score*

Right *By 1933 increasing personal mobility allowed more people to enjoy natural beauty spots*

Top *In the 1920s the char-à-banc outing brought the town dweller to the countryside*

Above *In 1928 the motorcycle was an important form of personal transport*

Above right *Picnic on the downs, 1936. The splendid Crossley car is of slightly earlier origin*

Right *The popular and inexpensive Ford open tourer in a typically suburban 1936 setting*

Above *The gramophone (a vintage specimen in this instance, even in 1925 when the picture was taken) was a popular source of home entertainment*

Right *By 1920 this veteran soldier was reduced to playing records in the street for money*

Above right *By the 1930s the portable gramophone had become for many as indispensable a companion for outings as today's transistor radio*

Far right *'Wireless' – 1927*

'Radio' – 1937. Throughout the 1930s many radio sets boasted cabinets of splendid design and finish such as this one

The seaside

The seaside ranks second only to the home as a setting for the snapshot. As early as 1903 the *Amateur Photographer* reported, 'At the seaside when the sun shines one person in ten carries a Kodak or some other form of hand camera . . . every errand boy and nursemaid carries one at the seaside'. In the early photographs there are relatively few showing people bathing, since this was not considered an entirely suitable subject for the camera until the early years of this century. These inhibitions were shed during the Edwardian era. Among the now almost vanished features of seaside life recorded in the snapshot are such entertainments as the pierrots, ventriloquists and Punch and Judy men, the goat carts and donkey rides, and the beach photographer with his portable darkroom and ferrotype pictures made in a minute, 'and fading almost as quickly'. Most of these were features of the seaside resort, and most have now fallen victim to their customers' increased sophistication and their preference for canned entertainments.

Top left *Despite the bedraggled wet bathing suit, the vivacity and charm of the subject are well portrayed in this 1901 picture*

Above left *A novel medium for advertising a familiar product, 1894*

Above *Aboard the Ducal yacht in 1901 – two pictures by Mary, Duchess of Bedford*

Top right *Brighton promenade, snapped in 1901 with the Kodak Panoram camera*

Centre right *The pierrot show on the sands, 1902*

Right *A 1900 mother and daughter resplendent in seaside lace and flowers*

Above *All the traditional ingredients of seaside amusement and entertainment are to be found in this picture of 1910. Note the bathing machines lined up at the water's edge*

Far left *An effective example of the oft-repeated theme of children on the beach*

Above left *The democracy of the beach – compare this picture with the bottom snapshot on page 87*

Left *The goat-cart excites interest, 1909*

Above left *Beach photographer with plenty of business, 1910*

Left *'Living Pictures' on the pier, 1912*

Above *Mrs Shaw and the bathing tent, taken by Shaw, 1912*

Above right *Beauty and the bathing machine at Eastbourne, Sussex, 1912*

Above *High jinks on the beach, 1914*

Right *The Shrimp Girl, 1918*

Above right *Another typical holiday scene with dad and the kids, 1914*

Far right *The ventriloquist entertains, 1920*

Left *A dynamic 1923 snapshot, full of life and movement*

Above *1925 Beach Parade*

Top *This Punch & Judy is playing to a capacity 1925 audience*

Above *Snapshooting in progress, 1930 with the subject in a characteristic pose!*

Above right *Donkey rides and laughter in 1934*

Right *'When Dad caught a crab that summer holiday in 1925'*

Far right *Inhibitions were discarded at the seaside. 1935*

Hollywood did much to sharpen the ordinary girl's awareness of style. 1939

Townscape

While the architecture of the town and city have been thoroughly recorded by the professional photographer, the people who live and work there tend to be subordinate in the postcard view. Indeed, the photographer frequently ensured, by choice of angle and time of day that the scene was not unduly cluttered with intrusive humanity. On the other hand, the urban scene is the background to many snapshots of people; human interest is predominant in the snapshot record. The snapshot captures the progressive change from horse-drawn traffic, with the army of crossing-sweepers needed to cope with the resulting filth to the motor vehicle, with the increasing congestion and danger it brought. The street vendors, pavement artists, shoeblacks and policemen, elegant and not so elegant passers-by are seen against a background of shopfronts, window displays and advertising hoardings, all of which provide invaluable detail for the social historian. The panoramic camera, with its wide angle of view, has recorded especially interesting views of the city scene.

Above *The Bowery in 1900, from the El station at Grand Street, New York*

Right *Refreshment stall at Finsbury Park, London, 1894*

Above right *A ginger-beer seller with his exotic canopied barrow, 1898*

Right *'Ask a policeman', 1905*

Far right *London flower girls, 1897*

Top *Two Kodak Panoram camera views of London:* top
Blackfriars; centre *Hyde Park Gate, 1902*

Above *Horse tram encounters herd of cows – not an uncommon
event in the Edwardian town, 1902*

Top left *The first Alexandra Rose day, one of the earliest hospital charity Flag Days in England, at St Martin in the Fields, London, 1912*

Top right *Magazine and newsvendors, 1911. Compare their printed headline notices with today's handwritten versions*

Above *Pavement artist at work, 1912*

Above *A variety of vehicles creates the traffic outside Victoria Station, London, 1915*

Above centre *A banner advertising an exhibition of Frank Brangwyn's etchings hangs above the shopfronts of fashionable New Bond Street, London, 1915*

Right *A matchseller, 1914*

Above right *This picture taken near the Royal Pavilion at Brighton, Sussex, in 1922 epitomises the relaxed pace of street life before the days of mass car ownership*

Far right *Rainy-day shopping in London's West End, 1932*

Above *'Stop me and buy one' – mobile ice-cream vendor*

Left *A 1936 street scene which is splendidly evocative of its era*

At work

Most of the early photographic records of people at work in towns and cities are the product of the professional photographer commissioned by industry. His task was to produce orderly and impressive studies of factory, mill or engine-shed, bearing testimony to the glory of the enterprises of which they formed a part. When the employees were included in such pictures, they were usually arranged in regimented rows by workbench, loom or machine, very much in the role of supporting characters. To some extent, the snapshot, with its emphasis on people, helps to redress the balance, off-setting this view of robot-like subservience. The countryman at work has been better documented by the amateur photographer, being rather more 'picturesque' than his urban counterpart. Working outdoors, he was also more easily photographed with the simple camera than was the factory or office worker in dim interiors.

Above, far left *Labourer at rest, 1901*

Above, centre left *Dipping sheep, 1902*

Far left *Road sweepers, essential workers in the big cities with their hundreds of thousands of horses, 1902*

Above *Rather self-conscious shoe-shine, 1902*

Above left *The fully equipped traditional chimney sweep, 1902*

Left *The rat-catcher, 1902*

Far left *Smokebox inspection, 1904*

Top *A road-mending scene of 1905 with no motor traffic to hinder progress*

Above left *Dust laying, 1912*

Above *Hay barge, 1930*

Left *On the plains, 1906*

Above *Fruit gathering, 1905*

Top right *Sowing, 1910*

Centre right *Homeward bound, 1908*

Bottom right *A scene taken in 1910 which can have changed little from previous centuries*

Far right, top *The blacksmith's shop, 1935. Another scene which must have remained constant for generations*

Far right, bottom *Threshing with a Crawley Brothers agricultural engine, 1906*

Telephoning in the office, an unusual setting for a portrait study

Interiors

Most snapshot cameras made during the first fifty years had provision for time exposures. With the camera resting on a solid support, the lens could be uncovered for long enough to record details of the interiors of room, including figures if they were patient enough to sit stock still for many seconds. Dim interiors could be lit by burning magnesium ribbon in one of the many cheap holders on sale; the more adventurous could use a magnesium powder flash lamp. After the introduction of the flashbulb and the Photoflood lamp in the early 1930s, most of the hazards and inconveniences were removed from interior photography.

The interiors of grander houses were sometimes photographed by professional photographers, and thus we have a record of their decor and furniture. The middle-class home was rarely documented by the professional and so the surviving snapshot records are all the more valuable. They show the clutter of the late Victorian and Edwardian eras slowly giving way to the sparser look of the 1920s and 1930s.

Top *Unusual panoramic view of a 1905 interior, taken with a No 1 Panoram Kodak camera*

Above *Five somewhat daunting American matrons, 1890*

Right *Ornately draped mantlepiece, 1902 – but it could have been twenty years earlier*

Far right, top *Mrs Patrick Campbell in bed – taken by George Bernard Shaw in 1907*

Centre right *Domestic harmony, 1902*

Far right *1903 cottage interior; the fireplace boasts a roasting-jack*

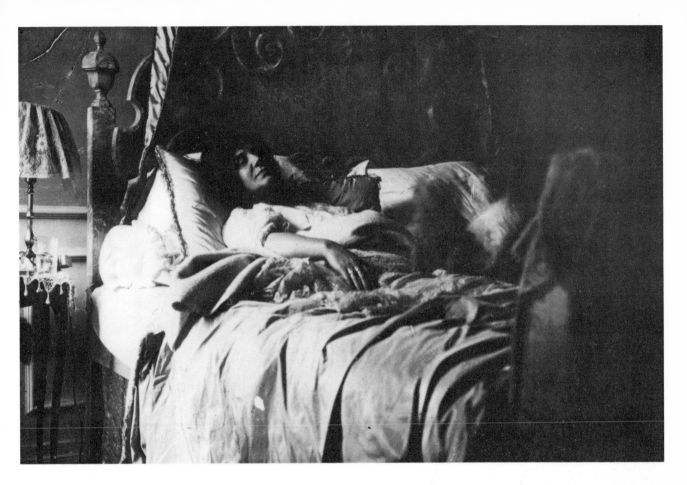

Above left *The 'cottage upright' piano was an essential symbol of lower-middle-class respectability in many a home. 1912*

Far left *By 1906 the draperies had gone from many mantlepieces, but the clutter of 'objets d'art' remained*

Centre left *Tobacconist's shop – a rare interior view of a small trader's premises in 1911*

Above *Aspidistra, armchair and lace curtain add to the charm of this 1910 portrait study*

Left *Measuring heights, 1912*

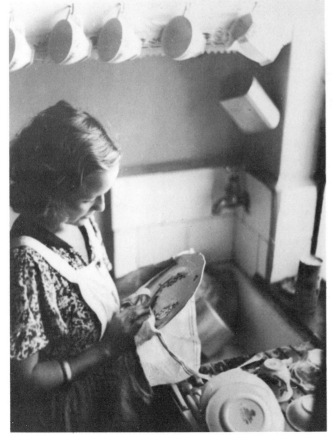

Far left, top *A 'comfortable' 1912 interior, with figures to match*

Far left, bottom *1920, but it could have been decades earlier. The bottle label states 'Rowntree's Lime Juice Cordial'.*

Above left *Dressed for the ball, 1929*

Above *Hearthside idyll, 1924*

Left *Compare with the photograph beyond. The girl is younger, the dress and hairstyle that of 1937, but the chore remains the same*

121

This 1938 interior study reveals the drastic simplification in living styles which had spread widely within a short span of years

Events

Until the arrival of the snapshot camera the ordinary person had no way to record the occasional dramatic events or famous people he encountered, except by writing about them, or by sketching, if he was so talented. The snapshot camera enabled the observer of notable events to record them as they happened. The soldier could become his own war correspondent; the Boer War was the first major conflict in which the ordinary soldier could carry a camera with him and many did. Despite regulations, many soldiers carried cameras with them on active service during the First World War. By concealing his camera, the soldier might be able to capture a front line scene, adding to the natural risks of war the risk of court martial if he were caught. More often, he recorded his comrades relaxing at camp behind the lines, clowning with each other to relieve tensions, or meeting the local inhabitants.

Events of less than world importance, but perhaps of even greater significance to the individual could be captured in the snapshot — family weddings, visiting celebrities, local happenings, all could be preserved in the family archives.

Top *In camp during the Boer War, South Africa, 1901*

Above *Another Boer War snapshot, 1901*

Top right *'The Toastmaster's Wedding', 1910*

Centre right *The Olympic Games, London, 1908. Dorando, later disqualified, running in the Marathon*

Right *Temperance meeting, 1906*

Above *An early submarine, photographed in 1912*

Right *The Paris Motor and Air show of 1911 featured both lighter-than-air as well as heavier-than-air craft*

Above right *King George V at Aldershot, Hampshire, 16th May, 1912*

Centre right *A protestor against the Women's Suffrage Movement, England, 1908*

Far right *Gladys Cooper, the celebrated actress, and companion sledding in 1912*

Far left *Recruiting, 1914*

Left *'Lewis Gunner Rowntree fighting off a Boche plane', 1918*

Centre left *'Kamerad' Light relief for British army officers indulging in a mock capture – 1916*

Bottom left *Tank on a country road, 1917*

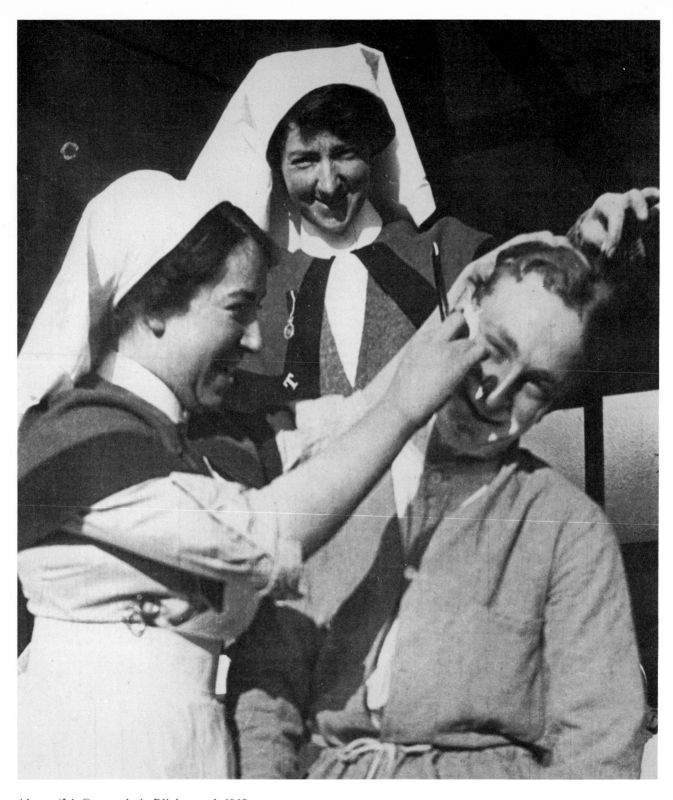

Above *'It's Great to be in Blighty . . .', 1918*

Above right *Lord Baden Powell, Chief Scout, inspects the Sea Scouts, 1936*

Right *Queen Mary inspects the Girl Guides, 1925*

Far right *Suzanne Lenglen and Helen Wills-Moody at Wimbledon in 1926*

Above left *A not uncommon accident to a ploughing engine, caused by a broken cable. 1910*

Far left *Malcolm Campbell standing in front of 'Bluebird' at Salt Flats, Utah, 1935*

Above *Fording the stream, 1924*

Left *Roadside catastrophe, 1935*

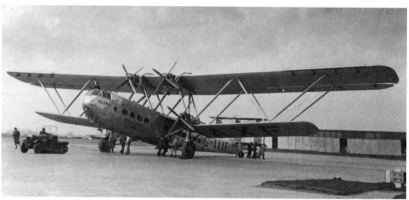

Top *Graf Zeppelin airship, 1931*

Above *Imperial Airways liner 'Helena'. Luxury air travel in a craft already sadly out of date by 1937 when this picture was taken*

Right *The RAF's 1935 Air Display at Hendon, Middlesex, featured a formation of fine vintage aircraft, with spectators' cars to match*

Glossary

Aperture In photography, the light-gathering capacity of the lens, usually expressed as an f/number, obtained by dividing the diameter of the lens opening into the focal length of the lens. Thus, a small f/number denotes a large lens opening and vice versa. Many earlier snapshot cameras had lenses calibrated in Uniform Series numbers; the Uniform Series numbers doubled as the aperture was halved — thus U.S.4 = f/8, U.S.8 = f/11, U.S.16 = f/16 and so on.

Cartridge roll film The conventional roll film, in which a length of sensitive film is attached to a longer length of black paper and wound on a spool. The paper protects the film from light and thus it can be loaded into the camera in daylight. The name was given from its similarity in shape to a shot-gun cartridge and its ease of loading into the camera.

Depth of field In theory, only one plane of the subject, that upon which the lens is focused, is sharply rendered in a photograph. In practice, objects before and behind this plane may also be rendered with adequate sharpness. The extent of this range of sharpness in the photograph is called depth of field. It is influenced by the lens aperture (*qv*) — a smaller aperture giving greater depth of field, by lens focal length (*qv*) — shorter focal length lenses, for a given aperture, having greater depth of field, and by focusing distance — the depth of field being less, for given aperture and focal length, for close subjects than for distant ones.

Development In photography, a process whereby an invisible, or latent, image, formed by brief exposure in the camera, is made visible on the film by chemical treatment.

Exposure The action of light upon the sensitive film. It is a function of time — controlled by the camera shutter (*qv*) and of intensity — controlled by the lens aperture (*qv*). The necessary exposure will vary with the prevailing lighting conditions, type of subject, and the sensitivity of the film.

Field of view The amount of the scene recorded on the sensitive film, usually expressed as an angle. A normal camera lens will embrace a field of view of about 45°.

Filter In photography, a disc or square of coloured glass or coloured gelatin, used to affect the tonal rendering of coloured objects in a black and white photograph. Used with an orthochromatic (*qv*) or panchromatic (*qv*) film, the filter will darken the rendering of objects of a complementary colour. Thus, a yellow filter will darken the rendering of a blue sky, heightening the contrast between sky and clouds.

Flash bulb A glass bulb containing magnesium or aluminium foil in an atmosphere of oxygen. When electrically ignited, the metal burns almost instantaneously, giving a brilliant but brief light. Flash bulbs came into general use around 1930, replacing the earlier, more hazardous and less controllable magnesium powder flash lamp.

f/number See 'Aperture'.

Focal length The distance a lens must be placed from a surface to form on it a sharp image of a subject at infinite distance.

Focal plane The position in the camera on which the lens is sharply focused and occupied by the film or plate.

Focusing The adjustment of the lens so as to give a sharp rendering of the subject on the film. It is usually done by moving the lens towards or away from the film, depending upon whether the subject is far or near. On simple cameras it may be done by adding an extra portrait or close-up lens to a fixed lens, so as to permit pictures of near subjects.

Gelatin dry plates Photographic materials derived from a process first suggested by Dr R. L. Maddox in 1871. The light-sensitive chemicals are carried in a layer of gelatin coated on the plate, a principle which has remained the basis of photography ever since.

Magnesium flash Magnesium powder, if blown through a hot flame such as that of a spirit lamp, will ignite and burn very rapidly, giving a brilliant white light. Such flash lamps were widely used in the 1880s and 1890s. Alternatively, the magnesium powder could be mixed with other chemicals, called oxidising agents, which enabled it to be ignited very readily by a taper, sparks from a flint wheel or by percussion caps. Flash lamps using this explosive mixture were popular during the earlier part of this century, until the advent of the flash bulb (*qv*).

Miniature camera A small camera taking negatives of small format. The 35mm film camera, popularised in the 1920s after the introduction of the Leica camera in 1925, influenced the development of small roll film cameras in the 1930s.

Orthochromatic A photographic material equally sensitive to blue, green and yellow light but not to red light.

Panchromatic A photographic material equally sensitive to all colours.

Photoelectric cell A layer of a light-sensitive metal, usually selenium, coated on an insulating base. When light falls on the cell, it generates an electric potential in proportion to the brightness of the illumination. This voltage can be measured by a galvanometer or meter to provide a basis for exposure calculation in photography.

Photoflood A trade name for a form of electric light bulb run from a voltage high enough to cause it to give out a very bright light, but with a greatly reduced life. The name is now loosely applied to all such lamps, regardless of manufacturer.

Portrait lens See 'Focusing'.

Rangefinder An optical device for measuring distance by a triangulation method based on a view of the subject from two separated lenses, whose images are combined in a single field. Rangefinders may be of the split-image type, in which the field is divided horizontally into two parts, one of which can be adjusted relative to the other by a calibrated control. When vertical lines appear unbroken across the field, the distance can be read from a scale. Other rangefinders use the coincidence method, in which two images appear superimposed until the correct distance is set, when they combine into one. Rangefinders can be directly coupled to the camera focusing control; the first camera to use this principle was the Autographic Kodak Special camera of 1916.

Roll holder A device containing a roll of sensitive material suitable for a number of exposures, replacing the conventional plate holder on a plate camera.

Shutter A mechanical device before, behind or between the lens elements normally excluding light from the camera, but which can be opened and closed for a controlled length of time to permit exposure of the sensitive material. Most simple box cameras have rotary shutters permitting only instantaneous exposures (of about 1/25 of a second) and time setting, in which the shutter can be held open for a long period. Folding cameras often have more complex shutters, permitting a range of longer or shorter exposure times.

Stripping paper or film An early form of roll film in which the sensitive layer could be removed from the paper base after exposure and development, and transferred to a transparent support for printing. It was made obsolete by the introduction of celluloid roll film in 1889.

Viewfinder A device to facilitate accurate aiming of the camera. Most snapshot cameras used small reflecting finders, in which a lens produced an image of the scene by means of a mirror on a small ground glass screen or in a clear lens. Some later cameras, particularly in the 1920s and 1930s, used frame viewfinders allowing the camera to be used at eye level.

Appendix: roll film sizes

After the introduction of the Vest Pocket Kodak camera in 1912, the Eastman Kodak Company adopted a new system of identifying the dozens of roll film sizes, which had previously been identified by the type of camera they fitted. With the great proliferation of camera models and film sizes, great confusion was possible. The Eastman Kodak Company adopted a numbering system, starting from 101, the numbers allocated in the order in which the various film sizes had been introduced originally. This numbering system was later taken up by most other manufacturers. A complete list of the Kodak roll film sizes up to 1939 is given below. Only a few sizes, 120, 620, 127 and 828, still survive.

Film number	Picture size (inches)	Introduced	Camera	Other Kodak cameras using this film size
101	3½×3½	1895	2 Bullet	2 Bull's-Eye (1896) 2 Falcon (1899) 2 Flexo (Plico) (1899) 2 Folding Pocket Kodak (1899) 2 Stereo Kodak (1901) Stereo Kodak Model 1 (1917)
102	1½×2	1895	Pocket Kodak	4 Bulls-Eye (1896)
103	4×5	1897	4 Bullet	4 Panoram Kodak (1899)
104	5×4	1897	4 Cartridge Kodak	
105	2¼×3¼	1897	1 Folding Pocket Kodak	1 Panoram Kodak (1900)
106	3½×3½	1898	2 Eureka (Zenith)	
107	3¼×4¼	1898	Roll Holders for plate cameras	
108	4½×3¼	1898	Roll Holders for plate cameras	
109	4×5	1898	Roll Holders for plate cameras	4 Eureka (Zenith) (1899)
110	5×4	1898	Roll Holders for plate cameras	
111	6½×4¾	1898	Roll Holders for plate cameras	
112	7×5	1898	Roll Holders for plate cameras	
113	9×12cm	1898	Roll Holders for plate cameras	
114	12×9cm	1898	Roll Holders for plate cameras	
115	7×5	1898	5 Cartridge Kodak	
116	2½×4¼	1899	1A Folding Pocket Kodak	2A Brownie (1907) 1A Speed Kodak (1909) 2A Folding Brownie (1910) Six-Three Kodak 1A (1913) 1A Kodak Jr. (1914) 1A Autographic Kodak (1914) 2A Folding Autographic Brownie (1915) 1A Kodak series II (1923) 1A Pocket Kodak series III (1924) 1A Pocket Kodak (1926)

Film number	Picture size (inches)	Introduced	Camera	Other Kodak cameras using this film size
117	2¼×2¼	1900	1 Brownie	
118	3¼×4¼	1900	3 Folding Pocket Kodak	Six-Three Kodak 3 (1913) 3 Autographic Kodak (1914) 3 Pocket Kodak series III (1926)
119	3¼×4¼	1900	3 Cartridge Kodak	
120	2¼×3¼	1901	2 Brownie	2 Folding Brownie 1904 1 Kodak Jr (1914) 1 Autographic Kodak Jr (1914) 1 Pocket Kodak series II (1922) 1 Pocket Kodak series III (1926) 1 Pocket Kodak (1926) 2 Beau Brownie (1930)
121	1⅝×2½	1902	0 Folding Pocket Kodak	
122	3¼×5½	1903	3A Folding Pocket Kodak	3A Folding Brownie (1909) Six-Three Kodak 3A (1913) 3A Autographic Kodak (1914) 3A Folding Autographic Brownie (1916) 3A Panoram Kodak (1926) 3A Pocket Kodak (1927) 3A Kodak series II (1936)
123	4×5	1904	4 Screen Focus Kodak	4 Folding Kodak (1907)
124	3¼×4¼	1905	3 Folding Brownie	3 Brownie (1908) 3 Bull's-Eye (1913)
125	3¼×5½	1905	2 Stereo Brownie	3B Quick Focus Kodak (1906)
126	4¼×6½	1906	4A Folding Kodak	4A Speed Kodak (1908)
127	1⅝×2½	1912	Vest Pocket Kodak	0 Brownie (1914) Vest Pocket Kodak Model B (1925) Vest Pocket Kodak series III (1926) Baby Brownie (1934) Jiffy VP (1935) Hawkeye Ace (1936) Bullet (1936)
128	2¼×1½	1913	1 Ensignette	
129	3×2	1913	2 Ensignette	
130	2⅞×4⅞	1916	2C Autographic Kodak	2C Folding Autographic Brownie (1916) 2C Pocket Kodak series III (1924) 2C Pocket Kodak (1925)
616	2½×4¼	1932	Kodak Six-16	Six-16 Brownie (1933) Jiffy Six-16 (1933) Kodak Senior Six-16 (1937)
620	2¼×3¼	1932	Kodak Six-20	Six-20 Brownie (1933) Jiffy Kodak Six-20 (1933) Kodak Senior Six-20 (1937) Super Kodak Six-20 (1938)
828	28×40mm	1935	Kodak Bantam	Kodak Bantam Special (1936)

Index

Bibliography

So far, little else has been published on the theme of this book. However, the reader interested in the general history of photography may find the following books of interest:

Coe, Brian, *The Birth of Photography*, Ash & Grant, London, 1976; Taplinger, New York, 1977
George Eastman and the Early Photographers, Priory Press, London, 1973

Gernsheim, Helmut & Alison, *The History of Photography*, Thames & Hudson, London, 1969; Aperture, Millerton, NY, 1973
A Concise History of Photography, Thames & Hudson, London, 1965; Grosset & Dunlap, New York, 1965

Newhall, Beaumont, *The History of Photography*, Museum of Modern Art, New York and New York Graphic Society, Greenwich, Conn., 1972; Secker & Warburg, London, 1973

The role of the photograph in historical research is dealt with in:

Martin, G. H. and Francis, David, 'The Camera's Eye' in *The Victorian City: Images and Reality*, ed. H. J. Dyos & Michael Wolff, Routledge and Kegan Paul, London and Boston, 1973

In recent years many books have been published drawing on old photographs, including snapshots, for their illustrations. They include:

Winter, Gordon, *Past Positive*, Chatto & Windus, London, 1971, republished in paperback as *A Cockney Camera*, Penguin Books, London, 1973 and New York, 1974
A Country Camera, Penguin Books, London, 1973 and New York, 1974
The Golden Years 1903-1913, David & Charles, London, 1975

The large series on British history through old photographs published by Batsford, London, may also be of interest.